سورة الزمر

SOORAH AZ-ZUMAR
CHAPTER 39 OF THE NOBLE QURAN

RESOURCES FOR YOUR 30-DAY STUDY
OF THE COMMENTARY OF AL-IMAM AS-SA'DEE
WORKBOOK PREPARED BY: MOOSAA RICHARDSON

THIS COPY BELONGS TO:

Copyright © 1446 (2025) by Moosaa Richardson.

All rights reserved. No part of this publication may be reproduced, distributed, or transmitted in any form or by any means, including photocopying, recording, or other electronic or mechanical methods, without the prior written permission of the copyright holder, except in the case of brief quotations embodied in critical reviews and certain other noncommercial uses permitted by copyright law.

First Print (Paperback) Edition: Sha'baan 1446 (February 2025)

Richardson, Moosaa. (Author)

Harding, Gibril (Proofreader)

Soorah az-Zumar, Chapter 39 of the Noble Quran (Workbook) / Resources for Your 30-Day Study of the Commentary of al-Imam as-Sa'dee

ISBN: 979-8310052352

1. Nonfiction —Religion —Islam —Koran & Sacred Writings.

2. Nonfiction —Religion —Islam —General.

3. Nonfiction —Religion —Islam —Sunnism.

TABLE OF CONTENTS

PREFACE TO THE WORKBOOK	5
INTRODUCTION: ABOUT SOORAH AZ-ZUMAR & THESE LESSONS	11
PERSONAL PROGRESS TRACKER	12
LESSON 1: BEGINNING WITH TOWHEED (THE ONENESS OF ALLAH) [VERSES 1-2]	13
LESSON 2: POLYTHEISTS AND THEIR INTERMEDIARIES [VERSE 3]	15
LESSON 3: THE ALMIGHTY CREATOR HAS NO SON OR PARTNER [VERSES 4-5]	17
LESSON 4: CONTEMPLATING ALLAH'S AMAZING CREATION [VERSE 6]	19
LESSON 5: INGRATITUDE LEADS TO THE HELLFIRE [VERSES 7-8]	21
LESSON 6: THE GREAT REWARD FOR PIETY AND PATIENCE [VERSES 9-10]	23
LESSON 7: THE GUIDING WORDS OF SINCERE WORSHIPPERS [VERSES 11-16]	25
LESSON 8: VIGILANCE, REPENTANCE, AND DUTIFUL COMPLIANCE [VERSES 17-18]	27
LESSON 9: THE VERDICT OF PUNISHMENT OR GREAT REWARDS [VERSES 19-20]	29
LESSON 10: PARABLES FOR THOUGHTFUL PEOPLE OF INSIGHT [VERSES 21-22]	31
LESSON 11: A BOOK OF GUIDANCE WITH AMAZING PARABLES [VERSE 23]	33
LESSON 12: WORLDLY DISGRACE AND UNENDING TORMENT [VERSES 24-26]	35
LESSON 13: ANOTHER PARABLE OF GUIDANCE FOR CONTEMPLATION [VERSES 27-31]	37
LESSON 14: HONESTY AND BELIEVING IN THE HONEST TRUTH [VERSES 32-35]	39
LESSON 15: ALLAH IS SUFFICIENT FOR THE FAITHFUL BELIEVERS [VERSES 36-38]	41
LESSON 16: OUR GOOD OR EVIL IS FOR OR AGAINST OURSELVES [VERSES 39-41]	43
LESSON 17: ALL INTERCESSION BELONGS TO ALLAH ALONE [VERSES 42-44]	45
LESSON 18: ALLAH'S JUDGMENT ON THE DAY OF RESURRECTION [VERSES 45-48]	47
LESSON 19: THE INGRATES OF MANKIND AND THEIR ARROGANCE [VERSES 49-52]	49
LESSON 20: NOT GIVING UP HOPE IN ALLAH'S VAST MERCY [VERSES 53-56]	51
LESSON 21: REGRET AND REMORSE WHEN IT IS TOO LATE [VERSES 57-59]	55
LESSON 22: YOU WILL SEE THEM ON THE DAY OF RESURRECTION [VERSES 60-61]	57
LESSON 23: THE UNCHALLENGED SOVEREIGNTY OF ALLAH [VERSES 62-63]	58
LESSON 24: CONFIDENT REFUSAL OF INVITATIONS TO FALSEHOOD [VERSES 64-66]	61
LESSON 25: LOFTY AND EXALTED ABOVE THE PARTNERS THEY CLAIM [VERSE 67]	63
LESSON 26: THE END OF THE WORLD AND THE LAST DAY [VERSES 68-70]	65
LESSON 27: DISBELIEVERS DRIVEN TOWARDS HELL IN GROUPS [VERSES 71-72]	67
LESSON 28: THE PIOUS ARRIVE AT THE GATES OF PARADISE [VERSE 73]	69
LESSON 29: HIS PROMISE IS KEPT: THE FAITHFUL INHERIT PARADISE [VERSE 74]	71
LESSON 30: ANGELS SURROUND THE THRONE EXALTING HIS PRAISE [VERSE 75]	73
A FINAL WORD	74
QUIZ I: REVIEW OF WEEK 1, LESSONS 1-8 (VERSES 1-16)	75
QUIZ 2: REVIEW OF WEEK 2, LESSONS 8-14 (VERSES 17-35)	77
QUIZ 3: REVIEW OF WEEK 3, LESSONS 15-21 (VERSES 36-59)	79
QUIZ 4: REVIEW OF WEEK 4, LESSONS 22-28 (VERSES 60-73)	81
QUIZ 5: COMPREHENSIVE FINAL EXAM (VERSES 1-75)	83
APPENDIX I: SOORAH AZ-ZUMAR & A TRANSLATION OF ITS MEANINGS	87
APPENDIX II: SOORAH AZ-ZUMAR (ARABIC PAGES FROM THE MUSHAF)	108

The First Muslim Mosque (Al-Masjid Al-Awwal), est. 1932, located in the heart of Pittsburgh's historic Hill District, hosts a vibrant community of local and international congregants, adhering to the tenets of Orthodox Sunni/Salafi Islam, actively condemning terrorist organizations such as ISIS, Alqaeda, and the (so-called) Muslim Brotherhood.

X/TWITTER: @1MMPGH

WEBSITE: WWW.FIRSTMUSLIMMOSQUE.COM

EMAIL: INFO@FIRSTMUSLIMMOSQUE.COM

بسم الله الرحمن الرحيم

PREFACE

In the Name of Allah, the Most Gracious, the Every Merciful. All praise is due to Allah, *al-Waahid* (the Uniquely Singular One), *al-Qahhaar* (the Ever Dominating One):

﴿خَلَقَ ٱلسَّمَٰوَٰتِ وَٱلۡأَرۡضَ بِٱلۡحَقِّ يُكَوِّرُ ٱلَّيۡلَ عَلَى ٱلنَّهَارِ وَيُكَوِّرُ ٱلنَّهَارَ عَلَى ٱلَّيۡلِۖ وَسَخَّرَ ٱلشَّمۡسَ وَٱلۡقَمَرَۖ كُلٌّ يَجۡرِي لِأَجَلٍ مُّسَمًّىۗ أَلَا هُوَ ٱلۡعَزِيزُ ٱلۡغَفَّٰرُ﴾ [الزُّمَر: ٥]

"He created the heavens and the earth, in truth. He makes the night merge into the day, and He makes the day merge into the night. He has made the sun and the moon to be of service [to mankind's needs]. **Each runs** [its course] **until a set time. Nay! He is the Almighty, the Oft-Forgiving."** [39:5]

It is He, the Lofty and Exalted, who sent down His Book of guidance, the Quran, to His noble Messenger, Muhammad ibn 'Abdillaah al-Haashimee (may Allah raise his rank and grant him peace), a Book of divine guidance and enlightenment for all who seek genuine piety and authentic knowledge, a Book of the finest discourse and the most intriguing parables, a Book that has the most profound effect on the believers, inwardly and outwardly, as Allah Himself has described it:

﴿ٱللَّهُ نَزَّلَ أَحۡسَنَ ٱلۡحَدِيثِ كِتَٰبًا مُّتَشَٰبِهًا مَّثَانِيَ تَقۡشَعِرُّ مِنۡهُ جُلُودُ ٱلَّذِينَ يَخۡشَوۡنَ رَبَّهُمۡ ثُمَّ تَلِينُ جُلُودُهُمۡ وَقُلُوبُهُمۡ إِلَىٰ ذِكۡرِ ٱللَّهِ﴾ [الزُّمَر: ٢٣]

"Allah has sent down the finest discourse, a familiar Book with parables of contrast, causing the skins of those who fear their Lord to shiver, and their skins and their hearts then soften to the remembrance of Allah…" [39:23]

May Allah, the Mighty and Majestic, make us from those who take this Quran as their guidance and embrace its study and implementation, those whose hearts surrender in humility to the Almighty who sent it, those who contemplate its rich parables of guidance, heed the reminders, and are led to noble doors of sincere piety in their worship of Allah:

﴿وَلَقَدۡ ضَرَبۡنَا لِلنَّاسِ فِي هَٰذَا ٱلۡقُرۡءَانِ مِن كُلِّ مَثَلٍ لَّعَلَّهُمۡ يَتَذَكَّرُونَ * قُرۡءَانًا عَرَبِيًّا غَيۡرَ ذِي عِوَجٍ لَّعَلَّهُمۡ يَتَّقُونَ﴾ [الزُّمَر: ٢٧ - ٢٨]

"We have put forth every type of parable for people in this Quran, so they could heed the reminder. An Arabic Quran, having no crookedness, so they could become pious." [39:28-29]

May He, the Ever Merciful and Gracious, make us from those He has described:

﴿ٱلَّذِينَ يَسۡتَمِعُونَ ٱلۡقَوۡلَ فَيَتَّبِعُونَ أَحۡسَنَهُۥۚ أُوْلَٰٓئِكَ ٱلَّذِينَ هَدَىٰهُمُ ٱللَّهُۖ وَأُوْلَٰٓئِكَ هُمۡ أُوْلُواْ ٱلۡأَلۡبَٰبِ﴾ [الزُّمَر: ١٨]

"Those who listen to the word and then follow the best of it who are the ones Allah has guided; it is they who are people of intellect." [39:18]

As for what follows: It is from the greatest of Allah's favors that we -once again- prepare for the blessed month of Ramadhaan, *in shaa' Allah*.

For many of us, these **"Ramadhaan Lessons"** have become an essential part of our experience, and I am -once again- humbled and honored to be part of your days and nights, asking Allah to accept from me and all of you. To briefly recount some of the many beautiful favors of Allah upon us over the last few years, as it relates to these lessons:

- **Volume 1** of this series was our study tool for the classes in Ramadhaan 1439 (2018). Thirty lessons consisted of seven modules each, with Grammar, *Tafseer*, and *Hadeeth* modules, as well as a variety of extension activities, beginning with the verses about fasting.
- **Volume 2** (1440/2019) included fifteen *Tafseer* lessons and fifteen *Hadeeth* lessons on various topics. A *fatwa* from Shaykh Ibn Baaz (may Allah have Mercy on him) was included in each lesson.
- **Volume 3** (1441/2020) included 30 lessons on each of the four main topics: *Tafseer, Hadeeth,* Arabic, and *Tajweed.* The 30 verses of **Soorah al-Mulk** were studied, one verse a day, for each day of the month, from **four** different books of *Tafseer*! Brief lessons in *Tajweed* and Arabic were also included.
- **Volume 4** (1442/2021) included another set of 120 lessons in *Tafseer, Hadeeth*, Arabic (*Sarf*, or word derivatives and conjugations), and *Tajweed,* focused on **Soorah Ibraaheem**. We cut back to reading **two** (not four) books of *Tafseer* – al-Baghawee and as-Sa'dee.
- **Volume 5** (1443/2022) included two lessons a day in study of **Soorah Ghaafir**, from those same two books of *Tafseer*.
- **Volume 6** (1444/2023) included daily studies of **Soorah al-Israa'**, reading the explanation of al-Imam as-Sa'dee (may Allah have Mercy on him).
- **Last year's Volume 7** (1445/2024) included a similar 30-day study of **Soorah al-Furqaan**, the 25th chapter of the Quran.

All seven of the previous workbooks remain available on Amazon and at many Islamic bookstores in different parts of the world, and to Allah Alone is the praise. Furthermore, the recordings from all those activities remain easily and freely accessible at al-Masjid al-Awwal's audio archives:

▶ ***www.Spreaker.com/user/radio1mm***

WHAT TO EXPECT IN THIS YEAR'S LESSONS

This workbook and this year's Ramadhaan 1446 (2025) classes will be a study of the amazing 39th chapter of the Quran, **Soorah az-Zumar**. Following last year's precedent, we will maintain a similar focus and scope throughout the lessons and workbook this year, *in shaa' Allah*, with 30 *Tafseer* lessons in total.

1. GETTING THE MOST OUT OF TAFSEER AS-SA'DEE

Our focused study of this one single book of *Tafseer* allows us to zoom in, getting more of a feel for the style and methodology of the amazing explanation of the great scholar, **al-Imam 'Abdur-Rahmaan ibn Naasir as-Sa'dee** (may Allah have Mercy on him).

2. LIVE DAILY BROADCASTS

As you expect from us, we provide live daily sessions throughout the month of Ramadhaan, broadcast right from our beloved masjid in Pittsburgh, the First Muslim Mosque, *in shaa' Allah*. The high-quality MP3 recordings of our live classes remain available for those who could not attend, to listen in whenever that is easy. *(Check out the easy visual guide on **page 10**, and on the back cover.)*

3. WEEKLY QUIZZES AND A FINAL EXAM

Following the previous years' precedent, this year's workbook also includes weekly quizzes and a final exam. After each week of lessons, you will have an opportunity to review and evaluate your understanding of that week's classes with a 10-question multiple-choice quiz, *in shaa' Allah*.

Additionally, a 25-question comprehensive final exam is available. These resources, along with a complete answer key, are found on **pages 75-86** of this workbook. (The answer key is found on **page 98**.)

4. A PERSONAL PROGRESS TRACKER

To help you manage all these resources and stay on track throughout the month, our uniquely designed **Personal Progress Tracker** provides more structure to your study. With it, you can track your daily progress and weekly quiz scores, *in shaa' Allah*. Adding in your final exam score after you review the month's lessons, you will get a total score out of 100 points. This helpful tool is found on **page 12** of this workbook.

SOME OF THE MAIN THEMES OF *SOORAH AZ-ZUMAR*

The *soorah* opens with an important reminder about the greatest miracle granted to the Prophet Muhammad (may Allah raise his rank and grant him peace), the revelation of the Noble Quran, a topic emphasized throughout the *soorah*. (See: Verses 23, 27-28, and 41.)

Then, we learn about many of the Names, Attributes and Actions of Allah through the first passages of the *soorah*, that He is **al-'Azeez** (the Almighty), **al-Hakeem** (the All Wise and Authoritative), **al-Waahid** (the Uniquely Singular One), **al-Qahhaar** (the Ever Dominating One), **al-Ghaffaar** (the Oft Forgiving), who guides, judges, wills, and creates. We learn about what pleases and displeases Him, and that He shall inform people about their actions on the Day of Judgment. We are reminded about His Mercy, and how He answers the prayers of His creation when they call upon Him alone, even from people who have committed the blasphemy of polytheism. (See: Verses 3-9.)

Similar to other early Makkan chapters of the Quran, *Soorah az-Zumar* includes a heavy focus on the Hereafter, descriptions of the believers and disbelievers, as well as vivid descriptions of Paradise and the Hellfire. *Taqwaa* (piety) is heavily stressed throughout the *soorah*, and many individual applications are provided, wherein we learn about specific virtues to aspire for, as well as specific sins and bad manners to avoid.

YET ANOTHER AMAZING WORKSHOP ON PERFECTING ONE'S CHARACTER

Making it especially impactful in Ramadhaan, our study of this *soorah*, similar to last year's study of *Soorah al-Furqaan*, equips us with essential steps for refining one's character and embodying the best of the manners which Allah loves, *in shaa' Allah*.

Good Traits to Embrace	Bad Character to Avoid
worshipping Allah alone	polytheism
sincerity	disbelief
gratitude	lying
devotion in one's worship	ingratitude
pious caution and fear	disobedience
hope and aspiration for good	losing track of oneself
intelligent contemplation	neglecting family
Ihsaan (proficiency in worship)	rejecting truth
patience	neglecting one's heart
hastening into goodness	oppression and wrongdoing
repentance	mockery of the truth
following the best of words	arrogance
being inclined towards good	ignorance
reliance upon Allah alone	
diligence and hard work	

DIVINE GUIDANCE WITH STEP-BY-STEP INSTRUCTIONS ON INVITING PEOPLE TO ISLAM

An especially interesting recurring theme of *Soorah az-Zumar* is the topic of dialogue between differing parties. Throughout this life, people will clash and differ with each other in all spheres of life. The most crucial and serious of clashes are those related to our purpose in life and how we are to fulfill it. These conversations are the most important interactions we encounter. Consider how Allah guides us through these crucial moments with detailed instructions:

﴿وَلَئِن سَأَلْتَهُم مَّنْ خَلَقَ ٱلسَّمَـٰوَٰتِ وَٱلْأَرْضَ لَيَقُولُنَّ ٱللَّهُ ۚ قُلْ أَفَرَءَيْتُم مَّا تَدْعُونَ مِن دُونِ ٱللَّهِ إِنْ أَرَادَنِيَ ٱللَّهُ بِضُرٍّ هَلْ هُنَّ كَـٰشِفَـٰتُ ضُرِّهِۦٓ أَوْ أَرَادَنِي بِرَحْمَةٍ هَلْ هُنَّ مُمْسِكَـٰتُ رَحْمَتِهِۦ ۚ قُلْ حَسْبِيَ ٱللَّهُ ۖ عَلَيْهِ يَتَوَكَّلُ ٱلْمُتَوَكِّلُونَ ۝ قُلْ يَـٰقَوْمِ ٱعْمَلُوا۟ عَلَىٰ مَكَانَتِكُمْ إِنِّي عَـٰمِلٌ ۖ فَسَوْفَ تَعْلَمُونَ ۝ مَن يَأْتِيهِ عَذَابٌ يُخْزِيهِ وَيَحِلُّ عَلَيْهِ عَذَابٌ مُّقِيمٌ ۝﴾ [الزُّمَر]

"And if you asked them: 'Who created the heavens and the earth?' They certainly say, 'Allah.' Say: 'Do you ever consider those you call upon besides Allah? If Allah decreed some harm to happen to me, could they remove His [decreed] harm? Or if He decreed some Mercy for me, could they withhold His Mercy?!' Say: 'Sufficient for me is Allah! In Him [alone] all those who rely [on someone] must place their trust.' Say: 'O my people! Perform your deeds as you do; I also perform deeds. Soon you shall come to know. The one whom punishment comes to, disgracing him, a never-ending punishment covers him.'" [39:38-40]

﴿قُلْ إِنِّيٓ أُمِرْتُ أَنْ أَعْبُدَ ٱللَّهَ مُخْلِصًا لَّهُ ٱلدِّينَ ۝ وَأُمِرْتُ لِأَنْ أَكُونَ أَوَّلَ ٱلْمُسْلِمِينَ ۝ قُلْ إِنِّيٓ أَخَافُ إِنْ عَصَيْتُ رَبِّي عَذَابَ يَوْمٍ عَظِيمٍ ۝ قُلِ ٱللَّهَ أَعْبُدُ مُخْلِصًا لَّهُۥ دِينِي ۝ فَٱعْبُدُوا۟ مَا شِئْتُم مِّن دُونِهِۦ ۗ قُلْ إِنَّ ٱلْخَـٰسِرِينَ ٱلَّذِينَ خَسِرُوٓا۟ أَنفُسَهُمْ وَأَهْلِيهِمْ يَوْمَ ٱلْقِيَـٰمَةِ ۗ أَلَا ذَٰلِكَ هُوَ ٱلْخُسْرَانُ ٱلْمُبِينُ ۝﴾ [الزُّمَر]

"Say: 'I have certainly been ordered to worship Allah, making the religion sincerely and purely for Him [alone]. And I have been commanded to be the first of the Muslims.' Say: 'I do indeed fear the punishment of a tremendous day, if I were to disobey my Lord.' Say: 'Allah is who I worship, making my religion purely and sincerely for Him [alone]. So worship whatever you want less than Him.' Say: 'Indeed, the losers are those who lose themselves and their families on the Day of Resurrection. Nay! Such is the [most] evident loss!'" [39:11-15]

These and many other intriguing and engaging topics make the study of this *soorah* -if Allah so wills- an absolutely incredible and life-changing experience. May Allah grant us understanding of His Majestic Book and sincere implementation of its uplifting guidance, and may He make us the first of those who submit and implement what they call to.

HOW TO ACCESS THE DAILY CLASSES

Go to **www.Spreaker.com/user/radio1mm** on your computer, phone, or smart device, and then scroll down on the main page under the title, **"PODCASTS"**. Click on **"1446 (2025) Ramadhaan Lessons,"** and you will then see a list of all available class recordings. Save the page's location or create a shortcut to it, so you can return to it easily. There is an easy visual guide which demonstrates exactly how you can access these free online classes on **page 10**.

NEW: Live broadcasts are available on the masjid's Mixlr channel (**www.mixlr.com/radion1mm**) every day, beginning at **5:30 pm EST** at the start of Ramadhaan, *in shaa' Allah*. Live class times will change weekly and shift significantly along with the change to Daylight Savings Time (EDT) on March 9, 2025, so pay attention to the masjid's X/Twitter announcements (**www.x.com/1MMPGH**).

PRINT OR ELECTRONIC EDITION?

These workbooks have been prepared to accompany our courses as traditionally printed paperback workbooks, available in hardcover editions as well. They have been adapted, secondarily, as Kindle print replicas and in PDF format. This is primarily for our brothers and sisters in different parts of the world who follow the classes but cannot obtain the printed versions in their location. Others may prefer the electronic versions, as they are more comfortable using tablets or other electronic devices. Without a device that allows easy notetaking, we highly recommend the print versions of the workbooks (paperback or hardcover).

GUIDED INSTRUCTION

As you likely already know, **our workbooks have not been designed for independent self-study.** To achieve the intended benefit from these lessons, attend our free online classes daily, or listen to the recordings whenever that is easy for you, and follow along using this workbook.

A WORD OF THANKS AND APPRECIATION

May Allah reward my ever-supportive wife and family, my beloved community at the First Muslim Mosque of Pittsburgh, my respected companion, Gibril Harding, for his helpful review, as well as Umm Abee Bakr, Umm 'Abdil-Qawee, Umm Maimoonah, Umm Sulaiman, and the rest of my Patreon family, and all of those who study with us and support these efforts, wherever they may be. I ask Allah that He grant me and all of you success in attaining His Pleasure and in drawing near to Him. May He raise the rank of his Messenger, Muhammad, and grant him and his family and companions peace.

**ABUL-'ABBAAS
MOOSAA RICHARDSON**
Education Director
First Muslim Mosque
Pittsburgh, Pennsylvania
Email: MR@bakkah.net
Twitter: @1MMeducation

مبارك عليكم الشهر

(Asking Allah to make this a blessed month for you.)

HOW TO ACCESS THE FREE CLASS RECORDINGS & AUDIO RESOURCES

Go to **www.Spreaker.com/user/radio1mm** on your computer, phone, or smart device, and then scroll down on the main page under the title, **"PODCASTS"** (as seen in the images above). Click on **"1446 (2025) Ramadhaan Lessons,"** and you will then see a list of all available class recordings and audio resources, *in shaa' Allah*. Save the page's location or create a shortcut to it, so you can return to it easily.

LIVE DAILY BROADCASTS (Starting at 5:30 pm EST at the start of Ramadhaan): www.mixlr.com/radio1mm

10

INTRODUCTION
ABOUT SOORAH AZ-ZUMAR & THESE LESSONS

ABOUT THE SOORAH

1. Its names, general theme & main topics
2. Is it *Makkee* or *Madanee*? And what is the difference?

ABOUT THESE LESSONS

3. Who was al-Imam as-Sa'dee?
4. About the *Tafseer* of as-Sa'dee
5. About these daily lessons

Serious students may use the following *Personal Progress Tracker* to monitor their completion of the course, as explained on page 7 in the *Preface*. Students who complete the course are encouraged to go back and review their memorization and understanding of the entire text every six months or so. Knowledge must be acquired with sincerity and reviewed often with diligence!

PERSONAL PROGRESS TRACKER

DAY	FOCUS OF STUDY	STUDIED	MEMORIZED	SCORE
1	SOORAH AZ-ZUMAR VERSES 1-2	☐ 0.5	☐ 0.5	___ / 1
2	SOORAH AZ-ZUMAR VERSE 3	☐ 0.5	☐ 0.5	___ / 1
3	SOORAH AZ-ZUMAR VERSES 4-5	☐ 0.5	☐ 0.5	___ / 1
4	SOORAH AZ-ZUMAR VERSE 6	☐ 0.5	☐ 0.5	___ / 1
5	SOORAH AZ-ZUMAR VERSES 7-8	☐ 0.5	☐ 0.5	___ / 1
6	SOORAH AZ-ZUMAR VERSES 9-10	☐ 0.5	☐ 0.5	___ / 1
7	SOORAH AZ-ZUMAR VERSES 11-16	☐ 0.5	☐ 0.5	___ / 1
●	QUIZ 1: LESSONS 1-7 (VERSES 1-16) & MEMORIZATION CHECK			___ / 10
8	SOORAH AZ-ZUMAR VERSES 17-18	☐ 0.5	☐ 0.5	___ / 1
9	SOORAH AZ-ZUMAR VERSES 19-20	☐ 0.5	☐ 0.5	___ / 1
10	SOORAH AZ-ZUMAR VERSES 21-22	☐ 0.5	☐ 0.5	___ / 1
11	SOORAH AZ-ZUMAR VERSE 23	☐ 0.5	☐ 0.5	___ / 1
12	SOORAH AZ-ZUMAR VERSES 24-26	☐ 0.5	☐ 0.5	___ / 1
13	SOORAH AZ-ZUMAR VERSES 27-31	☐ 0.5	☐ 0.5	___ / 1
14	SOORAH AZ-ZUMAR VERSES 32-35	☐ 0.5	☐ 0.5	___ / 1
●	QUIZ 2: LESSONS 8-14 (VERSES 17-35) & MEMORIZATION CHECK			___ / 10
15	SOORAH AZ-ZUMAR VERSES 36-38	☐ 0.5	☐ 0.5	___ / 1
16	SOORAH AZ-ZUMAR VERSES 39-41	☐ 0.5	☐ 0.5	___ / 1
17	SOORAH AZ-ZUMAR VERSES 42-44	☐ 0.5	☐ 0.5	___ / 1
18	SOORAH AZ-ZUMAR VERSES 45-48	☐ 0.5	☐ 0.5	___ / 1
19	SOORAH AZ-ZUMAR VERSES 49-52	☐ 0.5	☐ 0.5	___ / 1
20	SOORAH AZ-ZUMAR VERSES 53-56	☐ 0.5	☐ 0.5	___ / 1
21	SOORAH AZ-ZUMAR VERSES 57-59	☐ 0.5	☐ 0.5	___ / 1
●	QUIZ 3: LESSONS 15-21 (VERSES 36-59) & MEMORIZATION CHECK			___ / 10
22	SOORAH AZ-ZUMAR VERSES 60-61	☐ 0.5	☐ 0.5	___ / 1
23	SOORAH AZ-ZUMAR VERSES 62-63	☐ 0.5	☐ 0.5	___ / 1
24	SOORAH AZ-ZUMAR VERSES 64-66	☐ 0.5	☐ 0.5	___ / 1
25	SOORAH AZ-ZUMAR VERSE 67	☐ 0.5	☐ 0.5	___ / 1
26	SOORAH AZ-ZUMAR VERSES 68-70	☐ 0.5	☐ 0.5	___ / 1
27	SOORAH AZ-ZUMAR VERSES 71-72	☐ 0.5	☐ 0.5	___ / 1
28	SOORAH AZ-ZUMAR VERSE 73	☐ 0.5	☐ 0.5	___ / 1
●	QUIZ 4: LESSONS 22-28 (VERSES 60-73) & MEMORIZATION CHECK			___ / 10
29	SOORAH AZ-ZUMAR VERSE 74	☐ 0.5	☐ 0.5	___ / 1
30	SOORAH AZ-ZUMAR VERSE 75	☐ 0.5	☐ 0.5	___ / 1
●	QUIZ 5: COMPREHENSIVE FINAL EXAM (VERSES 1-75)			___ / 25
●	COMPREHENSIVE MEMORIZATION CHECK (VERSES 1-75)			___ / 5

TOTAL = _____ %

LESSON 1

BEGINNING WITH TOWHEED (THE ONENESS OF ALLAH)

TODAY'S VERSES

قال تعالى: بِسْمِ ٱللَّهِ ٱلرَّحْمَٰنِ ٱلرَّحِيمِ

﴿تَنزِيلُ ٱلْكِتَٰبِ مِنَ ٱللَّهِ ٱلْعَزِيزِ ٱلْحَكِيمِ ۝ إِنَّآ أَنزَلْنَآ إِلَيْكَ ٱلْكِتَٰبَ بِٱلْحَقِّ فَٱعْبُدِ ٱللَّهَ مُخْلِصًا لَّهُ ٱلدِّينَ ۝﴾

In the Name of Allah, the Most Gracious, the Ever Merciful.

1. [This is] Revelation of the Book from Allah, the Almighty, the Ever Wise and Authoritative.

2. Verily, We have sent down the Book to you, in truth, so worship Allah, as a sincere servant, making the [entire] Religion for Him [alone].

TAFSEER (EXPLANATION) OF THE VERSES

As your teacher reads the *Tafseer* of al-Imam as-Sa'dee (may Allah have Mercy on him), follow along carefully and take notes on the following points:

1. This *soorah* is *Makkiyyah* / *Madaniyyah*. (Circle one.) [Then summarize the differences.]

MAKKIYYAH	MADANIYYAH

[What Verses are exempted from this?]

2. What are the three basic topics being introduced here?

3. What are the meanings of these two Names of Allah?

AL-'AZEEZ	AL-HAKEEM

13

4. What can be deduced about the Quran from Allah's descriptions?

5. Who is referred to in the Verse, **"We have sent down the Book to YOU..."**?

6. What is the main goal of this noble revelation?

7. In what main ways is the Quran a book containing truth?

8. What is the obligation which all this leads to?

& THIS REQUIRES FROM US ➡

9. How can we fulfill Allah's Command in Verse 2?

LESSON 2

POLYTHEISTS AND THEIR INTERMEDIARIES

TODAY'S VERSE

قال تعالى:

3. Nay! Due to Allah [alone] is [all] sincere religiosity. Those who take protectors other than Him [say]: 'We only worship them to draw near to Allah, with more closeness.' Indeed, Allah shall judge between them about what they differ over. Indeed, Allah does not guide one who is a liar, an ingrate.

﴿أَلَا لِلَّهِ ٱلدِّينُ ٱلْخَالِصُ وَٱلَّذِينَ ٱتَّخَذُوا۟ مِن دُونِهِۦٓ أَوْلِيَآءَ مَا نَعْبُدُهُمْ إِلَّا لِيُقَرِّبُونَآ إِلَى ٱللَّهِ زُلْفَىٰٓ إِنَّ ٱللَّهَ يَحْكُمُ بَيْنَهُمْ فِى مَا هُمْ فِيهِ يَخْتَلِفُونَ إِنَّ ٱللَّهَ لَا يَهْدِى مَنْ هُوَ كَٰذِبٌ كَفَّارٌ ۝﴾

TAFSEER (EXPLANATION) OF THE VERSE

As your teacher reads the *Tafseer* of al-Imam as-Sa'dee (may Allah have Mercy on him), follow along carefully and take notes on the following points:

1. Regarding some basic meanings of this Verse:

    A. What previous meaning does it emphasize?

    B. What does it clarify?

    C. For whom is Allah pleased with this religion?

2. What are some of the most essential descriptions of this religion?

1.	4.
2.	5.
3.	

3. What are the real impacts of religions on human life?

A. *Towheed* ➡	
B. *Shirk* ➡	

15

4. So what did Allah ORDER, FORBID, and INFORM us about?

| ORDERED: | FORBADE: | INFORMED: |

5. What is the meaning of Allah's reference to them **"taking protectors"**?

6. How did the polytheists assume they were drawing near to Allah through intermediaries?

| | |

7. Otherwise, what did they know about the incapability of those objects of worship?

    A.   B.   C.

8. What erroneous analogy was at the core of their misguidance?

9. What are three different ways to consider the error of such an analogy?

    A.

    B.

    C.

10. How can basic contemplation about the Majesty of Allah distance one from these errors?

11. What three things can be deduced about those who make such errors?

| | | |

12. What does this say about the wisdom behind the prohibition of shirk?

13. What is Allah's actual verdict between them, as indicated in the Verse?

14. What does it mean when Allah does not guide someone?

15. How does a lying ingrate respond to guidance?

LESSON 3

THE ALMIGHTY CREATOR HAS NO SON OR PARTNER

TODAY'S VERSES

قال تعالى:

4. Had Allah wanted to have a son, He would have selected whomever He willed from those He has created; exalted He is! He is Allah, the Uniquely Singular One, the Ever Dominating One.

5. He created the heavens and the earth, in truth. He makes the night merge into the day, and He makes the day merge into the night. He has made the sun and the moon to be of service [to mankind's needs]. Each runs [its course] until a set time. Nay! He is the Almighty, the Oft-Forgiving.

﴿لَّوْ أَرَادَ ٱللَّهُ أَن يَتَّخِذَ وَلَدًا لَّٱصْطَفَىٰ مِمَّا يَخْلُقُ مَا يَشَآءُ ۚ سُبْحَٰنَهُۥ ۖ هُوَ ٱللَّهُ ٱلْوَٰحِدُ ٱلْقَهَّارُ ۝ خَلَقَ ٱلسَّمَٰوَٰتِ وَٱلْأَرْضَ بِٱلْحَقِّ ۖ يُكَوِّرُ ٱلَّيْلَ عَلَى ٱلنَّهَارِ وَيُكَوِّرُ ٱلنَّهَارَ عَلَى ٱلَّيْلِ ۖ وَسَخَّرَ ٱلشَّمْسَ وَٱلْقَمَرَ ۖ كُلٌّ يَجْرِى لِأَجَلٍ مُّسَمًّى ۗ أَلَا هُوَ ٱلْعَزِيزُ ٱلْغَفَّٰرُ ۝﴾

TAFSEER (EXPLANATION) OF THE VERSES

As your teacher reads the *Tafseer* of al-Imam as-Sa'dee (may Allah have Mercy on him), follow along carefully and take notes on the following points:

1. Who would claim or assume such a thing?

2. How would this non-reality have happened?

3. What is the meaning of **"Exalted He is"**?

4. What are the basic aspects of oneness found in the name, *al-Waahid*?

1.	3.
2.	4.

5. What logical problem is relative to the name, *al-Waahid*, when one claims there is a son?

17

6. What is the meaning of the name, *al-Qahhaar*?

7. What logical problem is relative to the name, *al-Qahhaar*, when one claims there is a son?

8. What benefit is found in the coupling of these two divine names together?

[REVIEW: The issue of pairing two names together from the book, *Exemplary Principles*.]

9. For what purpose were the heavens and earth created?

10. How is the day merged into the night, and vice-versa?

11. How are the sun and moon kept in their pathways?

12. What happens upon the arrival of the appointed time mentioned in the Verse?

13. What meanings of the name, *al-Azeez*, are apparent in this context?

14. What meanings of the name, *al-Ghaffaar*, are apparent in this context?

    (20:82)

LESSON 4

CONTEMPLATING ALLAH'S AMAZING CREATION

TODAY'S VERSE

قال تعالى:

6. He created you [all] from a single soul, and then He made for it its mate. He sent down for you eight kinds of cattle in pairs. He creates you in the wombs of your mothers, in stage after stage of formation, under three levels of darkness. Such is Allah, your Lord, to Him belongs the [entire] dominion. No one deserves worship other than Him, so how can you be turned away?

﴿خَلَقَكُم مِّن نَّفْسٍ وَاحِدَةٍ ثُمَّ جَعَلَ مِنْهَا زَوْجَهَا وَأَنزَلَ لَكُم مِّنَ ٱلْأَنْعَـٰمِ ثَمَـٰنِيَةَ أَزْوَٰجٍ يَخْلُقُكُمْ فِى بُطُونِ أُمَّهَـٰتِكُمْ خَلْقًا مِّنۢ بَعْدِ خَلْقٍ فِى ظُلُمَـٰتٍ ثَلَـٰثٍ ذَٰلِكُمُ ٱللَّهُ رَبُّكُمْ لَهُ ٱلْمُلْكُ لَآ إِلَـٰهَ إِلَّا هُوَ فَأَنَّىٰ تُصْرَفُونَ ۝﴾

TAFSEER (EXPLANATION) OF THE VERSE

As your teacher reads the *Tafseer* of al-Imam as-Sa'dee (may Allah have Mercy on him), follow along carefully and take notes on the following points:

1. How is this Verse connected to a previously mentioned divine name?

2. What conclusion of contrast can be drawn from the phrase, **"From a single soul"**?

3. What meanings can be recalled about the creation of the soul's mate?

4. What is the meaning of **"sending down"** cattle?

5. What exactly are the **"eight kinds of cattle in pairs"**?

    (6:143-144)

6. What is special about these animals, compared to other things Allah has provided?

19

7. What meaning is relative to the creation of people in the wombs of their mothers?

8. What relationship is emphasized with the mention of the stages of fetal development?

9. What are the three stages of darkness?

10. What three main things are referred to in the phrase, **"Such is Allah…"**?

      A.

      B.

      C.

11. How does the mention of Allah's Lordship connect back to one of His Names?

12. **"So how can you be turned away?"**

[PRINCIPLE: How the topic of lordship (*Ruboobiyyah*) leads into the topic of worship (*uloohiyyah*) throughout the Quran]

LESSON 5

INGRATITUDE LEADS TO THE HELLFIRE

قال تعالى:

TODAY'S VERSES

7. If you [all] disbelieve, Allah certainly remains without any need [for you]. He is not pleased with disbelief for His worshippers. If you are grateful, He is pleased with that for you. No one shall bear the burden of another. Then, unto your Lord is your return, and He informs you of what you had done. Indeed, He is All-Knowing about the realities of [people's] chests.

8. Whenever a harm reaches a person, he calls upon his Lord [alone], in repentance to Him. Then, when He returns His favor [of safety] back to him, he forgets what he supplicated about previously and sets up partners with Allah, in order to lead [himself and others] away from His Path. Say: 'Enjoy your disbelief for a moment; you will indeed be from the dwellers of the Fire.'

﴿إِن تَكْفُرُوا فَإِنَّ ٱللَّهَ غَنِيٌّ عَنكُمْ ۖ وَلَا يَرْضَىٰ لِعِبَادِهِ ٱلْكُفْرَ ۖ وَإِن تَشْكُرُوا يَرْضَهُ لَكُمْ ۗ وَلَا تَزِرُ وَازِرَةٌ وِزْرَ أُخْرَىٰ ۗ ثُمَّ إِلَىٰ رَبِّكُم مَّرْجِعُكُمْ فَيُنَبِّئُكُم بِمَا كُنتُمْ تَعْمَلُونَ ۚ إِنَّهُۥ عَلِيمٌۢ بِذَاتِ ٱلصُّدُورِ ۝ ۞ وَإِذَا مَسَّ ٱلْإِنسَٰنَ ضُرٌّ دَعَا رَبَّهُۥ مُنِيبًا إِلَيْهِ ثُمَّ إِذَا خَوَّلَهُۥ نِعْمَةً مِّنْهُ نَسِىَ مَا كَانَ يَدْعُوا إِلَيْهِ مِن قَبْلُ وَجَعَلَ لِلَّهِ أَندَادًا لِّيُضِلَّ عَن سَبِيلِهِۦ ۚ قُلْ تَمَتَّعْ بِكُفْرِكَ قَلِيلًا ۖ إِنَّكَ مِنْ أَصْحَٰبِ ٱلنَّارِ ۝﴾

TAFSEER (EXPLANATION) OF THE VERSES

As your teacher reads the *Tafseer* of al-Imam as-Sa'dee (may Allah have Mercy on him), follow along carefully and take notes on the following points:

1. How must we understand our own ingratitude and/or disbelief?

    A.

    B.

    C.

2. Why is Allah not pleased with the disbelief committed by His servants?

    A.

    B.

    C.

3. What kinds of gratitude are being referred to?

4. Why is Allah pleased with His worshipper's gratitude?

    A.

    B.

    C.

5. Since our behavior will not harm nor benefit Allah, what issue connects to this?

6. When is the return to our Lord?

7. How are our deeds known and made known on that day?

8. What is the meaning of the phrase, *"bi thaat as-sudoor"* (بذات الصدور)؟

9. What conclusion should we derive from this?

10. How can Verse 8 be summarized?

11. What kind of blessing is restored?

12. What was he supplicating about previously?

13. What is the meaning of associating partners in a way of misguidance?

14. Whom does Allah commands us to address in the last part of Verse 8?

15. Will their moments of relaxation and enjoyment actually do anything for them?

    (26:205-207)

LESSON 6

THE GREAT REWARD FOR PIETY AND PATIENCE

قال تعالى:

TODAY'S VERSES

9. Otherwise, what about someone devoutly obedient, in prostration at times at night and standing, worried about the Hereafter, hoping for the Mercy of his Lord? Say: 'Are those who know equal to those who do not know?' It is only the people of intellect who take admonition.

10. Say: 'O My worshippers who have believed, be pious unto Allah. Those who are piously proficient in this life shall have goodness. Allah's earth is spacious. It is only the patient ones who shall receive their reward without measure.'

﴿أَمَّنْ هُوَ قَانِتٌ ءَانَآءَ ٱلَّيْلِ سَاجِدًا وَقَآئِمًا يَحْذَرُ ٱلْءَاخِرَةَ وَيَرْجُواْ رَحْمَةَ رَبِّهِۦ ۗ قُلْ هَلْ يَسْتَوِى ٱلَّذِينَ يَعْلَمُونَ وَٱلَّذِينَ لَا يَعْلَمُونَ ۗ إِنَّمَا يَتَذَكَّرُ أُوْلُواْ ٱلْأَلْبَٰبِ ۝ قُلْ يَٰعِبَادِ ٱلَّذِينَ ءَامَنُواْ ٱتَّقُواْ رَبَّكُمْ ۚ لِلَّذِينَ أَحْسَنُواْ فِى هَٰذِهِ ٱلدُّنْيَا حَسَنَةٌ ۗ وَأَرْضُ ٱللَّهِ وَٰسِعَةٌ ۗ إِنَّمَا يُوَفَّى ٱلصَّٰبِرُونَ أَجْرَهُم بِغَيْرِ حِسَابٍ ۝﴾

TAFSEER (EXPLANATION) OF THE VERSES

As your teacher reads the *Tafseer* of al-Imam as-Sa'dee (may Allah have Mercy on him), follow along carefully and take notes on the following points:

1. How are the righteous described in Verse 9?

2. What three main things do people of knowledge know about?

    A.

    B.

    C.

3. How different are the knowledgeable from the ignorant?

4. When are the pious people most mindful?

5. What are the priorities of people of real intellect?

23

6. Comparatively, how do unintelligent people behave?

7. Who is to be addressed with this reminder in Verse 10; "Say..." (to whom)?

8. What are they being commanded to do?

9. What favor are they to be reminded about in this admonition?

10. What kind of pious proficiency (إحسان) are they involved in?

11. What specific kinds of goodness can they expect?		
A.	B.	C.
(16:97)		

13. What is implied by Allah's mention of the vastness of the earth?

14. How does this Verse address an assumption about the downtrodden?

15. What important hadeeth is relative to Verse 10?

16. What are the three types of patience?

    A.

    B.

    C.

17. What is the meaning of their reward being **"without measure"**?

18. What does this tell us about the virtue of patience?

LESSON 7

THE GUIDING WORDS OF SINCERE WORSHIPPERS

TODAY'S VERSES

قال تعالى:

11. Say: 'I have certainly been ordered to worship Allah, making the religion sincerely and purely for Him [alone].'

12. 'And I have been commanded to be the first of the Muslims.'

13. Say: 'I do indeed fear the punishment of a tremendous day, if I were to disobey my Lord.'

14. Say: 'Allah is who I worship, making my religion purely and sincerely for Him [alone].'

15. 'So worship whatever you want less than Him.' Say: 'Indeed, the losers are those who lose themselves and their families on the Day of Resurrection. Nay! Such is the [most] evident loss!'

16. They shall have coverings of Fire from above them, and coverings from below them as well. Such is how Allah strikes fear in His worshippers. O My worshippers! Be pious unto Me!

﴿قُلْ إِنِّي أُمِرْتُ أَنْ أَعْبُدَ ٱللَّهَ مُخْلِصًا لَّهُ ٱلدِّينَ ۝ وَأُمِرْتُ لِأَنْ أَكُونَ أَوَّلَ ٱلْمُسْلِمِينَ ۝ قُلْ إِنِّي أَخَافُ إِنْ عَصَيْتُ رَبِّي عَذَابَ يَوْمٍ عَظِيمٍ ۝ قُلِ ٱللَّهَ أَعْبُدُ مُخْلِصًا لَّهُ دِينِي ۝ فَٱعْبُدُوا۟ مَا شِئْتُم مِّن دُونِهِۦ ۗ قُلْ إِنَّ ٱلْخَٰسِرِينَ ٱلَّذِينَ خَسِرُوٓا۟ أَنفُسَهُمْ وَأَهْلِيهِمْ يَوْمَ ٱلْقِيَٰمَةِ ۗ أَلَا ذَٰلِكَ هُوَ ٱلْخُسْرَانُ ٱلْمُبِينُ ۝ لَهُم مِّن فَوْقِهِمْ ظُلَلٌ مِّنَ ٱلنَّارِ وَمِن تَحْتِهِمْ ظُلَلٌ ۚ ذَٰلِكَ يُخَوِّفُ ٱللَّهُ بِهِۦ عِبَادَهُۥ ۚ يَٰعِبَادِ فَٱتَّقُونِ ۝﴾

TAFSEER (EXPLANATION) OF THE VERSES

As your teacher reads the *Tafseer* of al-Imam as-Sa'dee (may Allah have Mercy on him), follow along carefully and take notes on the following points:

1. Who is to say this to whom?

2. What previous Verse does this command refer to?

3. Why should he be the first of the Muslims?

4. What is implied from stating that he was ordered with such?

25

5. How are his followers required to apply Islam?

6. What kind of disobedience is referred to?

7. Saying to them, **"Worship whatever you wish…"** reminds us of which *soorah*?

8. How can people "lose themselves"?

9. How do they lose their families on the Day of Resurrection?

10. How serious is such a loss?

11. What is the meaning of "coverings" of fire?

12. What does the word, **"Such"** (ذلك) refer to?

13. How does this scare and motivate people of piety?

14. What angles of divine care and concern does this passage illustrate?

      A.

      B.

      C.

      D.

      E.

      F.

LESSON 8

VIGILANCE, REPENTANCE, AND DUTIFUL COMPLIANCE

TODAY'S VERSES

قال تعالى:

17. Those who shun the worship of false deities and turn to Allah in repentance shall have glad tidings, so proclaim glad tidings to My worshippers!

18. It is those who listen to the word and then follow the best of it who are the ones Allah has guided; it is they who are people of intellect.

﴿وَٱلَّذِينَ ٱجْتَنَبُوا۟ ٱلطَّٰغُوتَ أَن يَعْبُدُوهَا وَأَنَابُوٓا۟ إِلَى ٱللَّهِ لَهُمُ ٱلْبُشْرَىٰ فَبَشِّرْ عِبَادِ ۝ ٱلَّذِينَ يَسْتَمِعُونَ ٱلْقَوْلَ فَيَتَّبِعُونَ أَحْسَنَهُۥٓ أُو۟لَٰٓئِكَ ٱلَّذِينَ هَدَىٰهُمُ ٱللَّهُ وَأُو۟لَٰٓئِكَ هُمْ أُو۟لُوا۟ ٱلْأَلْبَٰبِ ۝﴾

TAFSEER (EXPLANATION) OF THE VERSES

As your teacher reads the *Tafseer* of al-Imam as-Sa'dee (may Allah have Mercy on him), follow along carefully and take notes on the following points:

1. What is the connection between this passage and the previous one?

2. What is the meaning of *"taaghoot"* (الطاغوت) in this passage?

3. How does this address a potential error in identifying Allah's worshippers?

4. How do they turn to Allah in repentance?

5. How do their ambitions shift?

A. From: ⇨ To:

B. From: ⇨ To:

6. What kind of glad tidings shall they enjoy?

27

7. At what occasions are they given these glad tidings?

   A.

   B.

   C.

8. What is the greatest of these glad tidings in the Hereafter?

9. What deed is needed to deserve these glad tidings?

10. What kinds of words do they listen to? And how do they listen?

11. What does their selective application of some words say about them?

12. What are the best of all words, those most worthy of being followed?

13. What is the subtle connection between this passage and Verse 23?

14. What has Allah guided these believers to?

15. What important aspect of intellect do they possess?

16. What can be said about those who fail to distinguish between different statements?

17. What about someone who can distinguish, but does not follow the best of it?

LESSON 9

THE VERDICT OF PUNISHMENT OR GREAT REWARDS

TODAY'S VERSES

قال تعالى:

19. Yet the one upon whom the verdict of punishment rightfully applies, are you going to save him from the Fire?

20. But those who are pious unto their Lord shall have rooms, with rooms built above them, as rivers flow underneath them. A promise from Allah; Allah does not break His promise of reward.

﴿أَفَمَنْ حَقَّ عَلَيْهِ كَلِمَةُ ٱلْعَذَابِ أَفَأَنتَ تُنقِذُ مَن فِى ٱلنَّارِ ۝ لَـٰكِنِ ٱلَّذِينَ ٱتَّقَوْا۟ رَبَّهُمْ لَهُمْ غُرَفٌ مِّن فَوْقِهَا غُرَفٌ مَّبْنِيَّةٌ تَجْرِى مِن تَحْتِهَا ٱلْأَنْهَـٰرُ ۖ وَعْدَ ٱللَّهِ ۖ لَا يُخْلِفُ ٱللَّهُ ٱلْمِيعَادَ ۝﴾

TAFSEER (EXPLANATION) OF THE VERSES

As your teacher reads the *Tafseer* of al-Imam as-Sa'dee (may Allah have Mercy on him), follow along carefully and take notes on the following points:

1. Why do some people deserve the verdict of punishment upon them?

2. How do we understand this rhetorical question?

3. What kind of honor do the people of piety deserve?

4. What makes these **ghuraf** (rooms) special?

5. What is the meaning of **"rooms with rooms built above them"**?

6. How are these rooms **"built"**?

    A.

    B.

    C.

29

7. What details are understood from rivers flowing underneath the rooms?

8. What is the significance of this being something promised by Allah?

9. What does this indicate about what is expected and required from us?

LESSON 10

PARABLES FOR THOUGHTFUL PEOPLE OF INSIGHT

قال تعالى:

TODAY'S VERSES

21. Have you not seen that Allah sends down water from the sky, and then causes it to take paths down into the ground? Then, He brings forth from it vegetation of various colors. Then, it withers, and you see it turn yellow, and then He makes it become straw. Indeed, there is a reminder in that for people of intellect.

22. Or [consider] the one whom Allah expands his breast to accept Islam, and so he is upon a light from his Lord. So then woe to those whose hearts have hardened from the remembrance of Allah! Such are in manifest misguidance.

﴿أَلَمْ تَرَ أَنَّ ٱللَّهَ أَنزَلَ مِنَ ٱلسَّمَآءِ مَآءً فَسَلَكَهُۥ يَنَٰبِيعَ فِى ٱلْأَرْضِ ثُمَّ يُخْرِجُ بِهِۦ زَرْعًا مُّخْتَلِفًا أَلْوَٰنُهُۥ ثُمَّ يَهِيجُ فَتَرَىٰهُ مُصْفَرًّا ثُمَّ يَجْعَلُهُۥ حُطَٰمًا ۚ إِنَّ فِى ذَٰلِكَ لَذِكْرَىٰ لِأُو۟لِى ٱلْأَلْبَٰبِ ۞ أَفَمَن شَرَحَ ٱللَّهُ صَدْرَهُۥ لِلْإِسْلَٰمِ فَهُوَ عَلَىٰ نُورٍ مِّن رَّبِّهِۦ ۚ فَوَيْلٌ لِّلْقَٰسِيَةِ قُلُوبُهُم مِّن ذِكْرِ ٱللَّهِ ۚ أُو۟لَٰٓئِكَ فِى ضَلَٰلٍ مُّبِينٍ ۞﴾

TAFSEER (EXPLANATION) OF THE VERSES

As your teacher reads the *Tafseer* of al-Imam as-Sa'dee (may Allah have Mercy on him), follow along carefully and take notes on the following points:

1. How can Verse 21 be summarized?

2. How is it that rainwater takes paths down into the ground?

3. What are four examples of different kinds of vegetation?

4. When does the vegetation wither?

5. What is the meaning of *"hutaam"* (حطام)?

31

6. What can people of intellect deduce from this about the following topics?

    A. Allah's Mercy

    B. Allah's Power

    C. His right to be worshipped alone

7. TAKE A MOMENT TO SUPPLICATE WITH THE AUTHOR'S SUPPLICATION.

O Allah! Make us from the people of intellect, those whom You have made it a point to mention, those whom You have guided through the intellects you gave them and shown them the sublime knowledge of Your Book and the deep meanings of Your Verses, things which others do not grasp. It is You alone who is the Ever-Bestowing.	اللَّهُمَّ اجْعَلْنَا مِنْ أُولِي الْأَلْبَابِ الَّذِينَ نَوَّهْتَ بِذِكْرِهِمْ، وَهَدَيْتَهُمْ بِمَا أَعْطَيْتَهُمْ مِنَ الْعُقُولِ، وَأَرَيْتَهُمْ مِنْ أَسْرَارِ كِتَابِكَ وَبَدِيعِ آيَاتِكَ مَا لَمْ يَصِلْ إِلَيْهِ غَيْرُهُمْ، إِنَّكَ أَنْتَ الوَهَّابُ.

8. What is the meaning of a person being upon a light from his Lord?

9. What part of Verse 22 indicates an intended contrast?

10. What does it mean that some hearts are hardened to the remembrance of Allah?

11. What do such people deserve?

12. What four signs of true misery are found with misguided people?

    A.

    B.

    C.

    D.

LESSON 11

A BOOK OF GUIDANCE WITH AMAZING PARABLES

قال تعالى:

TODAY'S VERSE

23. Allah has sent down the finest discourse, a familiar Book with parables of contrast, causing the skins of those who fear their Lord to shiver, and their skins and their hearts then soften to the remembrance of Allah. Such is the guidance of Allah; He guides whomsoever He wills. And whomever Allah sends astray shall have no one to guide him.

﴿ٱللَّهُ نَزَّلَ أَحْسَنَ ٱلْحَدِيثِ كِتَٰبًا مُّتَشَٰبِهًا مَّثَانِىَ تَقْشَعِرُّ مِنْهُ جُلُودُ ٱلَّذِينَ يَخْشَوْنَ رَبَّهُمْ ثُمَّ تَلِينُ جُلُودُهُمْ وَقُلُوبُهُمْ إِلَىٰ ذِكْرِ ٱللَّهِ ذَٰلِكَ هُدَى ٱللَّهِ يَهْدِى بِهِۦ مَن يَشَآءُ وَمَن يُضْلِلِ ٱللَّهُ فَمَا لَهُۥ مِنْ هَادٍ ۝﴾

TAFSEER (EXPLANATION) OF THE VERSE

As your teacher reads the *Tafseer* of al-Imam as-Sa'dee (may Allah have Mercy on him), follow along carefully and take notes on the following points:

1. What is the main topic of this 23rd Verse?

2. What is the best discourse and the best of all revealed books?

3. What two conclusions about the Quran's contents can be drawn from this?

   A.

   B.

4. What about the Quran is **"familiar"** (متشابه)?

5. What is the deeper meaning of the Quran being *mutashaabih* (متشابه)?

6. What is another meaning of this same description from another Verse?

   (3:7)

7. What other phrase in this Verse proves this specific meaning of *mutashaabih* (متشابه)?

8. What is the meaning of the Quran being *mathaanee* (مثاني)?

1.	4.
2.	5.
3.	

9. What kind of wisdom is found in paired reminders and repetition?

10. How did this insightful awareness affect the author's approach in this book?

11. How does the content of the Quran impact believers?

12. Why does a believer's skin shiver?

13. Why do their hearts and skins then soften?

14. How does the Quran both motivate and scare a believer?

15. What does "such" (ذلك) refer to?

16. What is the significance of the guidance of Allah?

17. What is another possible meaning intended by the phrase, "such" (ذلك)?

18. Who are those whom Allah wants to guide?

(5:16)

19. How terrible is it to be abandoned by Allah and not guided?

20. What is the only outcome for someone who is not guided by Allah?

LESSON 12

WORLDLY DISGRACE AND UNENDING TORMENT

TODAY'S VERSES

قال تعالى:

﴿أَفَمَن يَتَّقِى بِوَجْهِهِۦ سُوٓءَ ٱلْعَذَابِ يَوْمَ ٱلْقِيَٰمَةِۚ وَقِيلَ لِلظَّٰلِمِينَ ذُوقُوا۟ مَا كُنتُمْ تَكْسِبُونَ ۝ كَذَّبَ ٱلَّذِينَ مِن قَبْلِهِمْ فَأَتَىٰهُمُ ٱلْعَذَابُ مِنْ حَيْثُ لَا يَشْعُرُونَ ۝ فَأَذَاقَهُمُ ٱللَّهُ ٱلْخِزْىَ فِى ٱلْحَيَوٰةِ ٱلدُّنْيَاۖ وَلَعَذَابُ ٱلْءَاخِرَةِ أَكْبَرُۚ لَوْ كَانُوا۟ يَعْلَمُونَ ۝﴾

24. Or [consider] the one who tries to ward off the punishment with his face on the Day of Resurrection! It shall be said to the oppressive ones: 'Taste what you have earned!'

25. Those before them had also disbelieved, and so the punishment came to them from where they could not even perceive.

26. So Allah made them taste the disgrace in this worldly life, and the punishment of the Hereafter is even greater, if they only knew!

TAFSEER (EXPLANATION) OF THE VERSES

As your teacher reads the *Tafseer* of al-Imam as-Sa'dee (may Allah have Mercy on him), follow along carefully and take notes on the following points:

1. What previously mentioned type of person is understood to be part of this comparison?

2. What kind of person does this Verse introduce?

3. What is the meaning of warding off the punishment with his face?

4. Who are the oppressive ones (الظالمين)?

5. In what manner is this statement said to them?

6. What comparison is introduced in Verse 25?

35

7. When did punishment overtake them?

8. How were they disgraced?

9. What lesson should modern disbelievers take from this reminder?

ATTENDING CLASSES WHILE IN I'TIKAAF (SECLUSION IN THE MASJID)

Some people may feel it is inappropriate to attend a class about Islam while performing *i'tikaaf* (seclusion in the masjid), which is commonly done in the last ten nights of Ramadhaan.

Our shaykh, the great scholar, **Muhammad ibn Saalih al-'Uthaymeen** (may Allah have Mercy on him) answered the following question:

QUESTION: Does it go against the spirit of *i'tikaaf* to busy oneself with seeking knowledge?

ANSWER: There is no doubt that seeking knowledge is an act of obedience to Allah. However, *i'tikaaf* has more to do with specific acts of obedience, such as prayer, remembrance, recitation of Quran, etc. There is no problem if the one performing *i'tikaaf* attends a lesson or two during the day or night, as this does not affect the (validity of) *i'tikaaf*. However, if the classes are continuous, and he begins reviewing (and focusing heavily on) his lessons, attending many sittings that distract him from his (more) personal acts of (private) worship, then no doubt, his *i'tikaaf* would be deficient. However, I do not hold that this invalidates his *i'tikaaf*. (**Source:** *ash-Sharh al-Mumti'*, 6/501)

LESSON 13

ANOTHER PARABLE OF GUIDANCE FOR CONTEMPLATION

TODAY'S VERSES

قال تعالى:

27. We have put forth every type of parable for people in this Quran, so they could heed the reminder.

28. An Arabic Quran, having no crookedness, so they could become pious.

29. Allah has provided the parable of a slave belonging to multiple owners in disagreement and another belonging to a single owner. Are they equal in comparison? All praise is due to Allah, yet most of them do not know.

30. Indeed, you are dead, and they are also certainly all dead.

31. Then, on the Day of Resurrection, you will all certainly be in the presence of your Lord, disputing with one another.

﴿وَلَقَدْ ضَرَبْنَا لِلنَّاسِ فِي هَٰذَا ٱلْقُرْءَانِ مِن كُلِّ مَثَلٍ لَّعَلَّهُمْ يَتَذَكَّرُونَ ۝ قُرْءَانًا عَرَبِيًّا غَيْرَ ذِي عِوَجٍ لَّعَلَّهُمْ يَتَّقُونَ ۝ ضَرَبَ ٱللَّهُ مَثَلًا رَّجُلًا فِيهِ شُرَكَآءُ مُتَشَٰكِسُونَ وَرَجُلًا سَلَمًا لِّرَجُلٍ هَلْ يَسْتَوِيَانِ مَثَلًا ٱلْحَمْدُ لِلَّهِ بَلْ أَكْثَرُهُمْ لَا يَعْلَمُونَ ۝ إِنَّكَ مَيِّتٌ وَإِنَّهُم مَّيِّتُونَ ۝ ثُمَّ إِنَّكُمْ يَوْمَ ٱلْقِيَٰمَةِ عِندَ رَبِّكُمْ تَخْتَصِمُونَ ۝﴾

TAFSEER (EXPLANATION) OF THE VERSES

As your teacher reads the *Tafseer* of al-Imam as-Sa'dee (may Allah have Mercy on him), follow along carefully and take notes on the following points:

1. What kind of parables are found in the Quran?

2. What is the intended wisdom behind these parables?

3. What is the significance of the Quran being in Arabic?

4. What is the meaning of the Quran having no crookedness?

5. What conclusion is logically drawn from this?

(18:1-2)

6. How has Allah made the path of piety easy for His worshippers?

7. What is the topic of the comparison mentioned in Verse 29?

8. What situation does the slave with multiple masters face?

9. What situation does the slave with a single master face?

10. What is the goal of the rhetorical question, **"Are they equal…?"**

11. Comparatively, what situation does a polytheist experience with his multiple gods?

12. What situation does a person of towheed experience?

13. What specific favor should one think of when reading, **"Al-hamdu lillaah"**?

14. How are we all dead, as Allah describes us in Verse 30?

    (21:34)

15. What will our dispute be about on the Day of Resurrection?

16. How are all matters resolved on that day?

    (58:6)

LESSON 14

HONESTY AND BELIEVING IN THE HONEST TRUTH

قال تعالى:

TODAY'S VERSES

32. Who is more oppressive than one who lies upon Allah and rejects the honest truth when it comes to him? Is not Jahannam a suitable abode for the disbelievers?

33. And the one who comes with the honest truth and believes in it [himself], such are the pious ones.

34. They shall have whatever they wish for with their Lord; such is the recompense of the proficiently pious.

35. So that Allah would expiate for them the worst of what they did and reward them based on the best of what they had done.

﴿فَمَنْ أَظْلَمُ مِمَّن كَذَبَ عَلَى ٱللَّهِ وَكَذَّبَ بِٱلصِّدْقِ إِذْ جَآءَهُۥٓ أَلَيْسَ فِى جَهَنَّمَ مَثْوًى لِّلْكَـٰفِرِينَ ۝ وَٱلَّذِى جَآءَ بِٱلصِّدْقِ وَصَدَّقَ بِهِۦٓ أُوْلَـٰٓئِكَ هُمُ ٱلْمُتَّقُونَ ۝ لَهُم مَّا يَشَآءُونَ عِندَ رَبِّهِمْ ذَٰلِكَ جَزَآءُ ٱلْمُحْسِنِينَ ۝ لِيُكَفِّرَ ٱللَّهُ عَنْهُمْ أَسْوَأَ ٱلَّذِى عَمِلُوا۟ وَيَجْزِيَهُمْ أَجْرَهُم بِأَحْسَنِ ٱلَّذِى كَانُوا۟ يَعْمَلُونَ ۝﴾

TAFSEER (EXPLANATION) OF THE VERSES

As your teacher reads the *Tafseer* of al-Imam as-Sa'dee (may Allah have Mercy on him), follow along carefully and take notes on the following points:

1. What kind of wrongdoing is introduced in the opening of the 32nd Verse?

2. What are some examples of this evil behavior?

3. What other Verse also warns against this behavior in a more general way?

4. If this is the case for one who is ignorant, what about one who knows better?

5. How serious is rejecting a messenger of truth?

6. How serious is combining these two crimes?

7. How is this kind of *"thulm"* the worst of all sins?

   (31:13)

39

8. How is another comparison introduced?

9. In what way does this person come with the honest truth?

10. Who is included in the generality of this description?

11. What does the bringer of truth believe in?

12. What is the significance of bringing truth and also believing in it?

13. What do each of these two behaviors indicate?

⬜ ➡ ⬜
⬜ ➡ ⬜

14. Who is being referred to in the meaning of: **"Such are the pious ones"**?

15. How is *taqwaa* (piety) relative to these two matters?

16. What is included in **"whatever they wish for"**?

17. What is the meaning of being proficiently pious *(ihsaan)*?

18. Can one implement *ihsaan* in one's dealings with other than Allah?

19. What are the three categories of deeds as understood from the 35th Verse?

⬜ ➡ ⬜
⬜ ➡ ⬜
⬜ ➡ ⬜

20. Which sins are expiated because of their piety?

21. How does Allah recompense the good deeds of His worshippers?
    (4:40)

LESSON 15

ALLAH IS SUFFICIENT FOR THE FAITHFUL BELIEVERS

TODAY'S VERSES

قال تعالى:

36. Is not Allah sufficient for His worshipper? And yet they [try to] scare you with those less than Him! Whomever Allah sends astray shall have no one to guide him.

37. Whomever Allah guides shall have no one to lead him astray. Isn't Allah One who is Almighty, the Owner of [just] Retribution?

38. And if you asked them: 'Who created the heavens and the earth?' They certainly say, 'Allah.' Say: 'Do you ever consider those you call upon besides Allah? If Allah decreed some harm to happen to me, could they remove His [decreed] harm? Or if He decreed some Mercy for me, could they withhold His Mercy?!' Say: 'Sufficient for me is Allah! In Him [alone] all those who rely [on someone] must place their trust.'

﴿أَلَيْسَ ٱللَّهُ بِكَافٍ عَبْدَهُۥ وَيُخَوِّفُونَكَ بِٱلَّذِينَ مِن دُونِهِۦ وَمَن يُضْلِلِ ٱللَّهُ فَمَا لَهُۥ مِنْ هَادٍ ۝ وَمَن يَهْدِ ٱللَّهُ فَمَا لَهُۥ مِن مُّضِلٍّ أَلَيْسَ ٱللَّهُ بِعَزِيزٍ ذِى ٱنتِقَامٍ ۝ وَلَئِن سَأَلْتَهُم مَّنْ خَلَقَ ٱلسَّمَٰوَٰتِ وَٱلْأَرْضَ لَيَقُولُنَّ ٱللَّهُ قُلْ أَفَرَءَيْتُم مَّا تَدْعُونَ مِن دُونِ ٱللَّهِ إِنْ أَرَادَنِىَ ٱللَّهُ بِضُرٍّ هَلْ هُنَّ كَٰشِفَٰتُ ضُرِّهِۦٓ أَوْ أَرَادَنِى بِرَحْمَةٍ هَلْ هُنَّ مُمْسِكَٰتُ رَحْمَتِهِۦ قُلْ حَسْبِىَ ٱللَّهُ عَلَيْهِ يَتَوَكَّلُ ٱلْمُتَوَكِّلُونَ ۝﴾

TAFSEER (EXPLANATION) OF THE VERSES

As your teacher reads the *Tafseer* of al-Imam as-Sa'dee (may Allah have Mercy on him), follow along carefully and take notes on the following points:

1. What is the meaning of Allah being sufficient for His worshipper?

2. Which worshipper is being referred to?

3. How did Allah suffice him specifically?

4. What is intended by **"those less than Him"**?

5. What does their behavior say about them?

6. Why is there no hope for one whom Allah does not guide?

7. What is the meaning of the Name, *al-'Azeez*, in this context?

8. What is the meaning of Allah's retribution?

9. **"And if you asked them..."** – Who are they?

10. Will they mention their own objects of worship?

11. In what context should these words be said to them?

12. What is the meaning of **"Do you see...?"** (أفرأيتم)

13. How general is the phrase, **"some harm"**?

14. To what level is their ability to remove harm being assessed?

15. How general is the phrase, **"some mercy"**?

16. What will their reply be to this detailed question?

17. In what context is the final statement conveyed to them?

18. What is the meaning of **"Sufficient for me is Allah! In Him** [alone] **all those who rely** [on someone] **must place their trust"**?

LESSON 16

OUR GOOD OR EVIL IS FOR OR AGAINST OURSELVES

قال تعالى:

TODAY'S VERSES

39. Say: 'O my people! Perform your deeds as you do; I also perform deeds. Soon you shall come to know.'

40. 'The one whom punishment comes to, disgracing him, a never-ending punishment covers him.'

41. Indeed, we have sent down to you the Book, for mankind, in truth. Whoever embraces guidance, that is for his own soul. Whoever strays only strays into harm against himself. And you are not a keeper in charge of them!

﴿قُلْ يَـٰقَوْمِ ٱعْمَلُوا۟ عَلَىٰ مَكَانَتِكُمْ إِنِّى عَـٰمِلٌۭ ۖ فَسَوْفَ تَعْلَمُونَ ۝ مَن يَأْتِيهِ عَذَابٌۭ يُخْزِيهِ وَيَحِلُّ عَلَيْهِ عَذَابٌۭ مُّقِيمٌ ۝ إِنَّآ أَنزَلْنَا عَلَيْكَ ٱلْكِتَـٰبَ لِلنَّاسِ بِٱلْحَقِّ ۖ فَمَنِ ٱهْتَدَىٰ فَلِنَفْسِهِۦ ۖ وَمَن ضَلَّ فَإِنَّمَا يَضِلُّ عَلَيْهَا ۖ وَمَآ أَنتَ عَلَيْهِم بِوَكِيلٍ ۝﴾

TAFSEER (EXPLANATION) OF THE VERSES

As your teacher reads the *Tafseer* of al-Imam as-Sa'dee (may Allah have Mercy on him), follow along carefully and take notes on the following points:

1. Who is being commanded to make this statement?

2. What does, **"Perform your deeds as you do,"** mean?

3. What kind of deeds does the caller do?

4. What shall they soon come to know about?

5. When does this disgrace befall them?

6. When does the never-ending punishment cover them?

43

7. What is the meaning of the description of the punishment, that it is *"muqeem"*?

8. What prevents them from rectifying themselves?

9. What are three main elements found in the Book?

    A.

    B.

    C.

10. What does it mean to embrace guidance?

11. When is misguidance harmful to the degree mentioned in this Verse?

12. To whom is one's misguidance harmful?

13. What is the meaning of the negation of being a keeper over the people?

14. What deduction can be made about the opposite of this negation?

LESSON 17

ALL INTERCESSION BELONGS TO ALLAH ALONE

قال تعالى:

TODAY'S VERSES

42. Allah takes the souls at the time of their death, and [the souls of] those who have not [yet] died, while they sleep. He keeps the one He has decreed death for and releases the other, until a set time. Indeed, in that are signs for a people who reflect.

43. Or have they taken those less than Allah as intercessors? Say: 'What if they do not possess any ability, nor have any intellect at all?'

44. Say: 'To Allah [alone] belongs all intercession. To Him belong the dominion of the heavens and the earth, and then back to Him you shall all be returned.'

﴿ٱللَّهُ يَتَوَفَّى ٱلْأَنفُسَ حِينَ مَوْتِهَا وَٱلَّتِى لَمْ تَمُتْ فِى مَنَامِهَا ۖ فَيُمْسِكُ ٱلَّتِى قَضَىٰ عَلَيْهَا ٱلْمَوْتَ وَيُرْسِلُ ٱلْأُخْرَىٰٓ إِلَىٰٓ أَجَلٍ مُّسَمًّى ۚ إِنَّ فِى ذَٰلِكَ لَءَايَـٰتٍ لِّقَوْمٍ يَتَفَكَّرُونَ ۝ أَمِ ٱتَّخَذُوا۟ مِن دُونِ ٱللَّهِ شُفَعَآءَ ۚ قُلْ أَوَلَوْ كَانُوا۟ لَا يَمْلِكُونَ شَيْـًٔا وَلَا يَعْقِلُونَ ۝ قُل لِّلَّهِ ٱلشَّفَـٰعَةُ جَمِيعًا ۖ لَّهُۥ مُلْكُ ٱلسَّمَـٰوَٰتِ وَٱلْأَرْضِ ۖ ثُمَّ إِلَيْهِ تُرْجَعُونَ ۝﴾

TAFSEER (EXPLANATION) OF THE VERSES

As your teacher reads the *Tafseer* of al-Imam as-Sa'dee (may Allah have Mercy on him), follow along carefully and take notes on the following points:

1. What is the overall meaning of Verse 42?

2. What kind of death is the first one mentioned?

3. Who takes the people's souls when they die, Allah or His angels?

    (32:11)

    (6:61)

4. How do we understand how Allah's taking of the souls includes His angels doing it?

5. What is the second kind of death, the lesser death?

45

6. What happens to one's soul during sleep?

7. Which soul does He keep?

8. Which soul does He release, and until when?

9. What do contemplative people reflect about, based on this context?

10. What insight into the hidden realities of the soul does this Verse provide?
    A.
    B.

11. What is the overall topic of Verses 43 and 44?

12. With what overall goal is this message conveyed to them?

13. Who is being referred to in the Verse, **"What if they do not possess any ability…"**?

14. How general is the intended negation of not owning anything?

15. As they do not have intellect, what is understood about those who worship them?

16. How do we understand that all intercession belongs to Allah?

17. What information in the verse further emphasizes this exclusivity?

18. What things are generally found in the heavens and on earth?

19. What is the required action based on the overall lesson of the Verse?

20. What happens when we return to Allah?

LESSON 18

ALLAH'S JUDGMENT ON THE DAY OF RESURRECTION

TODAY'S VERSES

قال تعالى:

45. When Allah alone is mentioned, the hearts of those who do not believe in the Hereafter are disgusted, yet when those less than Him are mentioned, they suddenly rejoice!

46. Say: 'O Allah! Creator of the heavens and earth, Knower of [both] the world of the unseen and that of observable affairs, You judge between Your worshippers in all that they have differed over.'

47. Had those who committed injustices owned all that is on earth in its entirety, and another [earth] similar to it, they would certainly offer that as ransom from the terrible punishment of the Day of Resurrection. And what Allah has for them becomes clear to them, what they had not been considering.

48. And the evils of what they earned become clear to them, as what they used to ridicule surrounds them.

﴿وَإِذَا ذُكِرَ ٱللَّهُ وَحْدَهُ ٱشْمَأَزَّتْ قُلُوبُ ٱلَّذِينَ لَا يُؤْمِنُونَ بِٱلْآخِرَةِ ۖ وَإِذَا ذُكِرَ ٱلَّذِينَ مِن دُونِهِۦ إِذَا هُمْ يَسْتَبْشِرُونَ ۝ قُلِ ٱللَّهُمَّ فَاطِرَ ٱلسَّمَٰوَٰتِ وَٱلْأَرْضِ عَٰلِمَ ٱلْغَيْبِ وَٱلشَّهَٰدَةِ أَنتَ تَحْكُمُ بَيْنَ عِبَادِكَ فِى مَا كَانُوا۟ فِيهِ يَخْتَلِفُونَ ۝ وَلَوْ أَنَّ لِلَّذِينَ ظَلَمُوا۟ مَا فِى ٱلْأَرْضِ جَمِيعًا وَمِثْلَهُۥ مَعَهُۥ لَٱفْتَدَوْا۟ بِهِۦ مِن سُوٓءِ ٱلْعَذَابِ يَوْمَ ٱلْقِيَٰمَةِ ۚ وَبَدَا لَهُم مِّنَ ٱللَّهِ مَا لَمْ يَكُونُوا۟ يَحْتَسِبُونَ ۝ وَبَدَا لَهُمْ سَيِّـَٔاتُ مَا كَسَبُوا۟ وَحَاقَ بِهِم مَّا كَانُوا۟ بِهِۦ يَسْتَهْزِءُونَ ۝﴾

TAFSEER (EXPLANATION) OF THE VERSES

As your teacher reads the *Tafseer* of al-Imam as-Sa'dee (may Allah have Mercy on him), follow along carefully and take notes on the following points:

1. How do the polytheists behave when they are invited to *towheed*?

2. Who are **"those less than Him"**?

3. How do the polytheists behave when their objects of worship are mentioned?

4. What outcome shall they face?

5. What is the meaning of **"Faatir"** (فاطر)?

6. What is the **"ghayb"** (الغيب), or unseen?

7. How detailed is the differing between people of *towheed* and people of *shirk*?

8. What is another Verse that elaborates on the parties involved in this differing?

    (22:17)

9. What more details are provided in *Soorah al-Hajj*?

    (22:19)

    (22:20)

    (22:21)

    (22:22)

    (22:23)

10. What are the two outcomes in the Hereafter?

    (6:82)

    (5:72)

11. What connections between Allah's Attributes are understood from Verse 46?

    A.

    B.

    C.

    (67:14)

12. How does this lead into Verse 47?

13. What is the meaning of *"soo' al-'athaab"* (سوء العذاب)?

14. What Verses from *Soorah ash-Shu'araa'* emphasize this reality?

    (26:88-89)

15. What is it that **"they had not even been considering"**?

16. What are **"the evils of what they earned"**?

17. What shall encompass them at that point?

LESSON 19

THE INGRATES OF MANKIND AND THEIR ARROGANCE

TODAY'S VERSES

قال تعالى:

49. When harm reaches a person, he calls out to Us, yet later after We deliver him back to Our blessings, he says: 'I was only given this because of knowledge.' Rather, it is a trial, yet most of them do not know.

50. Indeed, this was already said by those before them. Yet, all that they had earned would not suffice them.

51. So the evils of what they earned befell them. And those who committed injustice from among them shall have the evils of what they earn befall them, too, and they shall not escape.

52. Do they not know that Allah extends the provisions for whomsoever He wills and lessens it [for others]. Indeed, there are signs in that for people who believe.

﴿فَإِذَا مَسَّ ٱلْإِنسَٰنَ ضُرٌّ دَعَانَا ثُمَّ إِذَا خَوَّلْنَٰهُ نِعْمَةً مِّنَّا قَالَ إِنَّمَآ أُوتِيتُهُۥ عَلَىٰ عِلْمٍۭ بَلْ هِىَ فِتْنَةٌ وَلَٰكِنَّ أَكْثَرَهُمْ لَا يَعْلَمُونَ ۝ قَدْ قَالَهَا ٱلَّذِينَ مِن قَبْلِهِمْ فَمَآ أَغْنَىٰ عَنْهُم مَّا كَانُوا۟ يَكْسِبُونَ ۝ فَأَصَابَهُمْ سَيِّـَٔاتُ مَا كَسَبُوا۟ وَٱلَّذِينَ ظَلَمُوا۟ مِنْ هَٰٓؤُلَآءِ سَيُصِيبُهُمْ سَيِّـَٔاتُ مَا كَسَبُوا۟ وَمَا هُم بِمُعْجِزِينَ ۝ أَوَلَمْ يَعْلَمُوٓا۟ أَنَّ ٱللَّهَ يَبْسُطُ ٱلرِّزْقَ لِمَن يَشَآءُ وَيَقْدِرُ إِنَّ فِى ذَٰلِكَ لَءَايَٰتٍ لِّقَوْمٍ يُؤْمِنُونَ ۝﴾

TAFSEER (EXPLANATION) OF THE VERSES

As your teacher reads the *Tafseer* of al-Imam as-Sa'dee (may Allah have Mercy on him), follow along carefully and take notes on the following points:

1. What reality of mankind is exposed in Verse 49?

2. In what manner does he call out when in need?

3. What does he do once the blessings are restored?

4. What do they mean when they say, **"I was only given this because of knowledge"**?

5. How are blessings actually trials?

6. What does Verse 49 teach us about the ramifications of ignorance?

7. How are the polytheists of today just like those of the previous eras?

8. What are **"the evils of what they earn"** mentioned in Verse 51? (compared to Verse 48)

9. What is the difference between today's disbelievers and those of ancient times?

10. How is their assumption dismantled?

11. What is the meaning of **"yaqdiru" (يقدر)** in Verse 52?

12. What is the difference between Allah's distribution of wealth and faith?

13. What are some important lessons learned from this passage?

      A.

      B.

      C.

      D.

      E.

LESSON 20

NOT GIVING UP HOPE IN ALLAH'S VAST MERCY

TODAY'S VERSES

قال تعالى:

53. Say: 'O My worshippers who have wronged their own souls! Do not give up hope in the Mercy of Allah! Indeed, Allah forgives all sins; it is He who is Ever Forgiving, Ever Merciful.'

54. Repent to your Lord and surrender unto Him before the punishment comes to you, and then you would not be aided.

55. And follow the best of what was sent down to you from your Lord, before the punishment comes to you suddenly when you do not expect it.

56. Lest a person say: 'What a loss, that I have neglected matters regarding Allah; indeed I had been among those who mocked [the truth].'

﴿قُلْ يَـٰعِبَادِىَ ٱلَّذِينَ أَسْرَفُوا۟ عَلَىٰٓ أَنفُسِهِمْ لَا تَقْنَطُوا۟ مِن رَّحْمَةِ ٱللَّهِ ۚ إِنَّ ٱللَّهَ يَغْفِرُ ٱلذُّنُوبَ جَمِيعًا ۚ إِنَّهُۥ هُوَ ٱلْغَفُورُ ٱلرَّحِيمُ ۝ وَأَنِيبُوٓا۟ إِلَىٰ رَبِّكُمْ وَأَسْلِمُوا۟ لَهُۥ مِن قَبْلِ أَن يَأْتِيَكُمُ ٱلْعَذَابُ ثُمَّ لَا تُنصَرُونَ ۝ وَٱتَّبِعُوٓا۟ أَحْسَنَ مَآ أُنزِلَ إِلَيْكُم مِّن رَّبِّكُم مِّن قَبْلِ أَن يَأْتِيَكُمُ ٱلْعَذَابُ بَغْتَةً وَأَنتُمْ لَا تَشْعُرُونَ ۝ أَن تَقُولَ نَفْسٌ يَـٰحَسْرَتَىٰ عَلَىٰ مَا فَرَّطتُ فِى جَنبِ ٱللَّهِ وَإِن كُنتُ لَمِنَ ٱلسَّـٰخِرِينَ ۝﴾

TAFSEER (EXPLANATION) OF THE VERSES

As your teacher reads the *Tafseer* of al-Imam as-Sa'dee (may Allah have Mercy on him), follow along carefully and take notes on the following points:

1. In Verse 53, Allah informs:

WHO?	➡	
ABOUT WHAT?	➡	
ENCOURAGING WHAT?	➡	
BEFORE WHEN?	➡	

2. Who is being commanded to convey this to them?

3. How have they wronged their own souls?

4. What happens when people give up on the Mercy of Allah?

5. What are essential things to know about Allah, which prevent one from despair?

    A.

    B.

6. How do we understand the divine attributes of Forgiveness and Mercy?

7. How do we seek out Allah's Forgiveness and Mercy?

8. How can we actualize repentance and submissive surrender?

9. What is the difference between *inaabah* (إنابة) and *islaam* (إسلام)?

10. What other essential trait is derived from this guidance?

11. When is the deadline for these actions to be fulfilled?

12. How is Verse 54 a response to a question that could be asked?

13. What are some examples of the best things revealed which we can follow/implement?

14. What does one accomplish by fulfilling the above?

15. What is being encouraged by the warning about the coming punishment?

16. What happens if people continue in heedlessness without changing?

17. What is the meaning of the phrase, *fee janbillaah* (في جنب الله)?

18. What time is being referred to when one says, **"I had been among those…"**?

19. What had they been mocking?

*THE FOLLOWING HADEETH STUDY IS NOT FROM THE TAFSEER OF AL-IMAM AS-SA'DEE.

On the authority of Ibn 'Abbaas (may Allah be pleased with him): Some of the people of polytheism had killed and fornicated much, so they came to Muhammad (may Allah raise his rank and grant him peace) and said, "Indeed, what you say and call to is great, but would you tell us if there is any expiation for the things we have done?" So then it was revealed, **"And those who do not call upon anyone along with Allah, nor do they kill any soul which Allah forbids to be violated, except by right, nor do they fornicate."** [25:68] Also, it was revealed: **"Say: 'O My worshippers who have wronged their own souls! Do not give up hope in the Mercy of Allah.'"** (39:53) [Agreed upon]

عَنِ ابْنِ عَبَّاسٍ ـ رَضِيَ اللهُ عَنْهُمَا ـ : أَنَّ نَاسًا مِنْ أَهْلِ الشِّرْكِ كَانُوا قَدْ قَتَلُوا وَأَكْثَرُوا، وَزَنَوْا وَأَكْثَرُوا، فَأَتَوْا مُحَمَّدًا ـ صَلَّى اللهُ عَلَيْهِ وَسَلَّمَ ـ ، فَقَالُوا: إِنَّ الَّذِي تَقُولُ وَتَدْعُو إِلَيْهِ لَحَسَنٌ، لَوْ تُخْبِرُنَا أَنَّ لِمَا عَمِلْنَا كَفَّارَةً؟ فَنَزَلَ: ﴿وَٱلَّذِينَ لَا يَدْعُونَ مَعَ ٱللَّهِ إِلَٰهًا ءَاخَرَ وَلَا يَقْتُلُونَ ٱلنَّفْسَ ٱلَّتِي حَرَّمَ ٱللَّهُ إِلَّا بِٱلْحَقِّ وَلَا يَزْنُونَ﴾ [الفُرْقَان: ٦٨]، وَنَزَلَتْ ﴿قُلْ يَٰعِبَادِيَ ٱلَّذِينَ أَسْرَفُوا۟ عَلَىٰٓ أَنفُسِهِمْ لَا تَقْنَطُوا۟ مِن رَّحْمَةِ ٱللَّهِ﴾ [الزُّمَر: ٥٣]. مُتَّفَقٌ عَلَيْهِ.

Points to consider from this hadeeth:

'Aa'ishah narrated that the Prophet (may Allah raise his rank and grant him peace) taught her to say when seeking *Laylat al-Qadr*, the Night of Qadr, the following supplication:

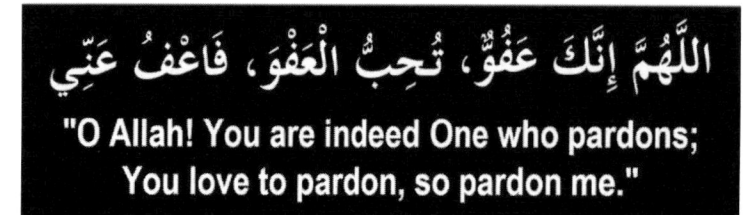

اللَّهُمَّ إِنَّكَ عَفُوٌّ، تُحِبُّ الْعَفْوَ، فَاعْفُ عَنِّي

"O Allah! You are indeed One who pardons; You love to pardon, so pardon me."

Collected by Ahmad, at-Tirmithee, and others. See: *Silsilat al-Ahaadeeth as-Saheehah* (no.3337).

LESSON 21

REGRET AND REMORSE WHEN IT IS TOO LATE

TODAY'S VERSES

قال تعالى:

﴿أَوْ تَقُولَ لَوْ أَنَّ ٱللَّهَ هَدَىٰنِى لَكُنتُ مِنَ ٱلْمُتَّقِينَ ۝ أَوْ تَقُولَ حِينَ تَرَى ٱلْعَذَابَ لَوْ أَنَّ لِى كَرَّةً فَأَكُونَ مِنَ ٱلْمُحْسِنِينَ ۝ بَلَىٰ قَدْ جَآءَتْكَ ءَايَـٰتِى فَكَذَّبْتَ بِهَا وَٱسْتَكْبَرْتَ وَكُنتَ مِنَ ٱلْكَـٰفِرِينَ ۝﴾

57. Or lest one say: 'Had Allah only guided me, I would have been among the pious.'

58. Or lest one say when he sees the punishment: 'If I only had another chance, I would be among the proficiently pious.'

59. Nay! Our Verses did indeed come to you, yet you disbelieved in them, behaved with arrogance, and became one of the disbelievers!

TAFSEER (EXPLANATION) OF THE VERSES

As your teacher reads the *Tafseer* of al-Imam as-Sa'dee (may Allah have Mercy on him), follow along carefully and take notes on the following points:

1. What is the meaning of the Arabic word, *"low"* (لو), in Verse 57?

2. Are they trying to excuse themselves because of Qadr?

3. What is the significance of actually seeing the punishment?

4. What is the meaning of the word, *"karrah"* (كرة) in Verse 58?

5. How can Allah's response to their false hopes be summarized?

6. What kind of *aayaat* came to them?

55

7. How did their arrogance affect their interaction with the truth?

8. Are claims about what they would do if given a second chance valid?

    (6:28)

LESSON 22

YOU WILL SEE THEM ON THE DAY OF RESURRECTION

قال تعالى:

TODAY'S VERSES

60. On the Day of Resurrection you will see those who lied on Allah, their faces will be darkened. Is not Jahannam the [suitable] abode of the arrogant?

61. Yet, Allah saves those who were pious, since they had taken the means of salvation; no harm touches them, nor do they grieve.

﴿وَيَوْمَ ٱلْقِيَٰمَةِ تَرَى ٱلَّذِينَ كَذَبُواْ عَلَى ٱللَّهِ وُجُوهُهُم مُّسْوَدَّةٌۚ أَلَيْسَ فِى جَهَنَّمَ مَثْوًى لِّلْمُتَكَبِّرِينَ ۝

وَيُنَجِّى ٱللَّهُ ٱلَّذِينَ ٱتَّقَوْاْ بِمَفَازَتِهِمْ لَا يَمَسُّهُمُ ٱلسُّوٓءُ وَلَا هُمْ يَحْزَنُونَ ۝﴾

TAFSEER (EXPLANATION) OF THE VERSES

As your teacher reads the *Tafseer* of al-Imam as-Sa'dee (may Allah have Mercy on him), follow along carefully and take notes on the following points:

1. Who sees the liars on the Day of Judgment with their faces darkened?

2. How can this treatment be described as something which matches their crime?

3. In what ways were they arrogant?

4. How could one respond to this rhetorical question?

5. What kinds of behavior are considered "lying on Allah"?

6. How does this passage exemplify the meaning of the Quran being *"mathaanee"*?

REVIEW: LESSON 11, QUESTION 8

7. What are **"the means of salvation"** which the pious have?

8. What is the *soo'* (السوء) mentioned in Verse 61?

9. What added level of reward is understood from them not being afraid?

10. How does this safety extend into the safety of *Daar as-Salaam*?

(35:34)

LESSON 23

THE UNCHALLENGED SOVEREIGNTY OF ALLAH

TODAY'S VERSES

قال تعالى:

62. Allah has created all things, and He is a watchful keeper over all things.

63. To Him belong the keys of the heavens and the earth. Those who disbelieve in the aayaat (i.e., signs and verses) of Allah are themselves the losers.

﴿ٱللَّهُ خَٰلِقُ كُلِّ شَيْءٍ وَهُوَ عَلَىٰ كُلِّ شَيْءٍ وَكِيلٌ ۝ لَّهُۥ مَقَالِيدُ ٱلسَّمَٰوَٰتِ وَٱلْأَرْضِ وَٱلَّذِينَ كَفَرُواْ بِـَٔايَٰتِ ٱللَّهِ أُوْلَٰٓئِكَ هُمُ ٱلْخَٰسِرُونَ ۝﴾

TAFSEER (EXPLANATION) OF THE VERSES

As your teacher reads the *Tafseer* of al-Imam as-Sa'dee (may Allah have Mercy on him), follow along carefully and take notes on the following points:

1. How do these descriptions of Allah connect to the topic of disbelief?

2. What does this oft-repeated description prove?

3. What do philosophers and some deviants say about some things?

4. Does Verse 62 support the argument of those who say the Quran is created?

5. What relationship between Allah and the universe is identified here?

6. What attributes can be understood from Allah being the *"Wakeel"* of all things?

    A.

    B.

    C.

7. What are the *"maqaaleed"* of the heavens and the earth?

(35:2)

8. What is the connection between Allah's attributes and the topic of disbelievers?

9. What do the *Aayaat* of Allah guide people to?

10. What are six major aspects of the loss which disbelievers suffer in the Hereafter?

*THE FOLLOWING HADEETH IS NOT FROM THE TAFSEER OF AL-IMAM AS-SA'DEE.

Chapter: "Say: Which of all things is the greatest testimony? Say: Allah [Himself]." [6:19] Allah, the Exalted, refers to Himself as a thing, and the Prophet (may Allah raise his rank and grant him peace) referred to the Quran as a thing, while it is one of Allah's Attributes. He also said, **"Everything shall perish, except for His Face." [28:88]**

بَابٌ: ﴿قُلْ أَيُّ شَيْءٍ أَكْبَرُ شَهَادَةً قُلِ اللَّهُ﴾ [الأنعام: ١٩]، فَسَمَّى اللهُ تَعَالَى نَفْسَهُ شَيْئًا، وَسَمَّى النَّبِيُّ ـ صَلَّى اللهُ عَلَيْهِ وَسَلَّمَ ـ الْقُرْآنَ شَيْئًا، وَهُوَ صِفَةٌ مِنْ صِفَاتِ اللهِ، وَقَالَ: ﴿كُلُّ شَيْءٍ هَالِكٌ إِلَّا وَجْهَهُ﴾ [القصص: ٨٨]

7417. 'Abdullaah ibn Yoosuf narrated to us, that Maalik informed us, from Aboo Haazim, from Sahl ibn Sa'd, that the Prophet (may Allah raise his rank and grant him peace) asked a man, **"Do you have anything with you of the Quran?"** He replied, "Yes, such-and-such *soorahs*," mentioning some *soorahs* specifically.

٧٤١٧ ـ حَدَّثَنَا عَبْدُاللهِ بْنُ يُوسُفَ، أَخْبَرَنَا مَالِكٌ، عَنْ أَبِي حَازِمٍ، عَنْ سَهْلِ بْنِ سَعْدٍ: قَالَ النَّبِيُّ ـ صَلَّى اللهُ عَلَيْهِ وَسَلَّمَ ـ لِرَجُلٍ: «أَمَعَكَ مِنَ الْقُرْآنِ شَيْءٌ؟» قَالَ: نَعَمْ، سُورَةُ كَذَا وَسُورَةُ كَذَا، لِسُوَرٍ سَمَّاهَا.

LESSON 24

CONFIDENT REFUSAL OF INVITATIONS TO FALSEHOOD

قال تعالى:

TODAY'S VERSES

64. Say: 'Is it other than Allah you order me to worship, O ignorant ones?'

65. He did indeed reveal to you and to all those before you, that if you were to commit polytheism, your deeds would certainly become null and void, and you would indeed be among the losers.

66. Instead, just worship Allah [alone], and be among the grateful.

﴿قُلْ أَفَغَيْرَ ٱللَّهِ تَأْمُرُوٓنِّىٓ أَعْبُدُ أَيُّهَا ٱلْجَٰهِلُونَ ۞ وَلَقَدْ أُوحِىَ إِلَيْكَ وَإِلَى ٱلَّذِينَ مِن قَبْلِكَ لَئِنْ أَشْرَكْتَ لَيَحْبَطَنَّ عَمَلُكَ وَلَتَكُونَنَّ مِنَ ٱلْخَٰسِرِينَ ۞ بَلِ ٱللَّهَ فَٱعْبُدْ وَكُن مِّنَ ٱلشَّٰكِرِينَ ۞﴾

TAFSEER (EXPLANATION) OF THE VERSES

As your teacher reads the *Tafseer* of al-Imam as-Sa'dee (may Allah have Mercy on him), follow along carefully and take notes on the following points:

1. Answer the following questions about Verse 64:

WHO IS TO SAY IT?	➡	
TO WHOM?	➡	
WHAT IS TO BE SAID?	➡	

2. Why are the disbelievers called "ignorant ones" in the Verse?

3. What are the worst consequences of polytheism?

4. Who are **"all those before you"**?

5. How does the language of the Verse indicate broad inclusion of all actions?

(6:88)

61

6. What kind of loss is suffered by those who commit polytheism?

7. What is the alternative provided in Verse 66?

8. What are some examples of things a person of *towheed* should be grateful for?

    A.

    B.

    C.

    D.

9. Which of Allah's blessings are the most important?

10. How does proper reflection over this topic resolve a serious character flaw?

وَالعُجْبَ فَاحْذَرْهُ إِنَّ العُجْبَ مُجْتَرِفٌ   أَعْمَالَ صَاحِبِهِ فِي سَيْلِهِ العَرِمِ

LESSON 25

LOFTY AND EXALTED ABOVE THE PARTNERS THEY CLAIM

قال تعالى:

TODAY'S VERSE

67. They did not form a proper estimate of Allah, like what is due to Him. The entire earth on the Day of Resurrection shall be in His grasp, and the heavens shall be rolled up in His right Hand. Exalted is He and lofty, above the partners they ascribe to Him.

﴿وَمَا قَدَرُواْ ٱللَّهَ حَقَّ قَدْرِهِۦ وَٱلْأَرْضُ جَمِيعًا قَبْضَتُهُۥ يَوْمَ ٱلْقِيَٰمَةِ وَٱلسَّمَٰوَٰتُ مَطْوِيَّٰتٌۢ بِيَمِينِهِۦ ۚ سُبْحَٰنَهُۥ وَتَعَٰلَىٰ عَمَّا يُشْرِكُونَ ۝٦٧﴾

TAFSEER (EXPLANATION) OF THE VERSE

As your teacher reads the *Tafseer* of al-Imam as-Sa'dee (may Allah have Mercy on him), follow along carefully and take notes on the following points:

1. Who are **"they"**, the ones who did not form a proper estimate?

2. What kind of estimate did they actually have for their idols?

3. What are some of the worst ramifications of this unjust consideration?

4. What is the meaning of **"Exalted is He and lofty"**?

63

***THE FOLLOWING HADEETH STUDY IS NOT FROM THE TAFSEER OF AL-IMAM AS-SA'DEE.**

On the authority of Aboo Hurayrah (may Allah be pleased with him): The Messenger of Allah (may Allah raise his rank and grant him peace) said, "Allah, the Blessed and Lofty, grabs the [entire] **earth on the Day of Judgment, and He rolls up the sky in His Right Hand**, and then He says, 'I am the King! Where are the kings of the earth?'" [Agreed upon]

عَنْ أَبِي هُرَيْرَةَ ـ رَضِيَ اللهُ عَنْهُ ـ، قَالَ: قَالَ رَسُولُ اللهِ ـ صَلَّى اللهُ عَلَيْهِ وَسَلَّمَ ـ : «يَقْبِضُ اللهُ ـ تَبَارَكَ وَتَعَالَى ـ الأَرْضَ يَوْمَ القِيَامَةِ، وَيَطْوِي السَّمَاءَ بِيَمِينِهِ، ثُمَّ يَقُولُ: أَنَا المَلِكُ! أَيْنَ مُلُوكُ الأَرْضِ؟» [مُتَّفَقٌ عَلَيْهِ]

Points to consider from this hadeeth:

CONNECTION: Review Module 9.5 from Ramadhaan Lessons, Vol.5 (1443).

LESSON 26

THE END OF THE WORLD AND THE LAST DAY

TODAY'S VERSES

قال تعالى:

68. That is when the horn shall be blown, and everyone in the heavens and everyone on earth collapses, save those whom Allah wills. Then, it shall be blown again, and all stand suddenly, looking around.

69. And the earth will then brighten by the light of its Lord. The Book will be set in place, and the prophets and witnesses are brought forth. They are judged by the truth, and they shall not be oppressed.

70. Each soul will be recompensed for what it did, as He knows best about what they had done.

﴿وَنُفِخَ فِى ٱلصُّورِ فَصَعِقَ مَن فِى ٱلسَّمَٰوَٰتِ وَمَن فِى ٱلْأَرْضِ إِلَّا مَن شَآءَ ٱللَّهُ ۖ ثُمَّ نُفِخَ فِيهِ أُخْرَىٰ فَإِذَا هُمْ قِيَامٌ يَنظُرُونَ ۝ وَأَشْرَقَتِ ٱلْأَرْضُ بِنُورِ رَبِّهَا وَوُضِعَ ٱلْكِتَٰبُ وَجِا۟ىٓءَ بِٱلنَّبِيِّـۧنَ وَٱلشُّهَدَآءِ وَقُضِىَ بَيْنَهُم بِٱلْحَقِّ وَهُمْ لَا يُظْلَمُونَ ۝ وَوُفِّيَتْ كُلُّ نَفْسٍ مَّا عَمِلَتْ وَهُوَ أَعْلَمُ بِمَا يَفْعَلُونَ ۝﴾

TAFSEER (EXPLANATION) OF THE VERSES

As your teacher reads the *Tafseer* of al-Imam as-Sa'dee (may Allah have Mercy on him), follow along carefully and take notes on the following points:

1. What is the benefit of this shift in topic?

2. What details do we know about the horn itself?

3. What details do we know about the one who blows the horn?

4. What is the meaning of the **"collapse"**?

5. What about the blowing of the horn causes them to collapse?

6. Who are exempted from collapsing?

7. What two names are used to refer to this first blowing of the horn?

8. What name is used to refer to the second blowing of the horn?

9. What is the situation of those standing up after the horn blows again?

10. Why are they looking around?

11. What can be understood from the brightening of the earth?

12. How can they withstand seeing Allah's light?

13. What book will be set in place?

(18:49)

14. What is said to the people regarding their books?

(17:14)

CONNECTION: Review Lesson 5 from Ramadhaan Lessons (1444): *Soorah al-Isaa'*.

15. Why are the prophets brought forward?

16. What kinds of witnesses are called forth?

17. What is the meaning of **"They are judged by the truth"**?

18. What is the judgment based on?

    A.

    B.

    C.

    D.

# LESSON 27

DISBELIEVERS DRIVEN TOWARDS HELL IN GROUPS

قال تعالى:

TODAY'S VERSES

71. And those who disbelieved will be driven towards Jahannam in groups. Then, when they arrive at it, its gates are opened, and its caretakers say to them: 'Did not messengers from among you come to you, reciting to you the verses of your Lord and warning you of the meeting on this day of yours?' They say: 'Of course, but the verdict of punishment is now justly applied to the disbelievers.'

72. It is said: 'Enter through the gates of Jahannam, abiding therein forever; what a terrible abode that is for the arrogant!'

﴿وَسِيقَ ٱلَّذِينَ كَفَرُوٓاْ إِلَىٰ جَهَنَّمَ زُمَرًاۖ حَتَّىٰٓ إِذَا جَآءُوهَا فُتِحَتْ أَبْوَٰبُهَا وَقَالَ لَهُمْ خَزَنَتُهَآ أَلَمْ يَأْتِكُمْ رُسُلٌ مِّنكُمْ يَتْلُونَ عَلَيْكُمْ ءَايَٰتِ رَبِّكُمْ وَيُنذِرُونَكُمْ لِقَآءَ يَوْمِكُمْ هَٰذَاۚ قَالُواْ بَلَىٰ وَلَٰكِنْ حَقَّتْ كَلِمَةُ ٱلْعَذَابِ عَلَى ٱلْكَٰفِرِينَ ۞ قِيلَ ٱدْخُلُوٓاْ أَبْوَٰبَ جَهَنَّمَ خَٰلِدِينَ فِيهَاۖ فَبِئْسَ مَثْوَى ٱلْمُتَكَبِّرِينَ ۞﴾

TAFSEER (EXPLANATION) OF THE VERSES

As your teacher reads the *Tafseer* of al-Imam as-Sa'dee (may Allah have Mercy on him), follow along carefully and take notes on the following points:

1. What is the result of the disbelievers separating themselves from the followers of truth?

2. What are the details of how they are driven towards Jahannam?

3. How can Jahannam be described in three basic ways?

    A.

    B.

    C.

4. Why are they pushed along?

    (52:13)

5. What kinds of groups are formed as they are pushed along?

6. How do they arrive at the gates of Jahannam?

7. In what tone or manner is their welcoming?

8. What does it mean that the messengers were **"from among you"**?

9. What *aayaat* were they reciting to them?

10. What was expected from them when their messengers warned them?

11. In what tone is their confession and acknowledgement?

12. What is the main cause of the verdict of punishment?

13. What tone is used when ordering them to enter Jahannam?

14. How do they enter through the gates?

15. What is the meaning of **"abiding therein forever"**?

16. How is their recompense perfectly suited to their actions?

    What was this verse revealed about?

    How broadly does it apply?

LESSON 28

THE PIOUS ARRIVE AT THE GATES OF PARADISE

قال تعالى:

TODAY'S VERSE

73. And those who were pious unto their Lord are led towards Paradise in groups. Then, when they arrive there, its gates are [soon] opened, and its caretakers say: 'Peace be upon you! You had been good, so come inside to abide forever!'

﴿وَسِيقَ ٱلَّذِينَ ٱتَّقَوۡاْ رَبَّهُمۡ إِلَى ٱلۡجَنَّةِ زُمَرًا ۖ حَتَّىٰٓ إِذَا جَآءُوهَا وَفُتِحَتۡ أَبۡوَٰبُهَا وَقَالَ لَهُمۡ خَزَنَتُهَا سَلَـٰمٌ عَلَيۡكُمۡ طِبۡتُمۡ فَٱدۡخُلُوهَا خَـٰلِدِينَ ۝﴾

TAFSEER (EXPLANATION) OF THE VERSE

As your teacher reads the *Tafseer* of al-Imam as-Sa'dee (may Allah have Mercy on him), follow along carefully and take notes on the following points:

1. How did these people practice piety unto Allah?

2. What is the difference in how the word, *"seeqa"* (سيق), is used for them?

3. What is their condition as they are being led along?

4. What situation do they encounter as they approach the gates?

5. In what mannerism are these gates opened for them?

6. What tone is used when greeting them?

7. What is the meaning of their greeting at the gates, **"Peace be upon you"**?

8. What does *tibtum* (طِبۡتُمۡ), **"You had been good,"** mean?

69

9. What does the letter **FAA'** in the phrase, **fad-khuloo** (فادخلوا), indicate?

10. What connection is there between their actions and the nature of this abode?

11. What is the difference between how the gates open at each of the two places?

12. What do the Verses prove about the uniqueness of these two places?

LESSON 29

HIS PROMISE IS KEPT: THE FAITHFUL INHERIT PARADISE

قال تعالى:

TODAY'S VERSE

74. They say: 'All praise is due to Allah, the One who kept his promise and made us to inherit this place, to dwell in Paradise wherever we want! How great is the reward of those who had worked [for it]!'

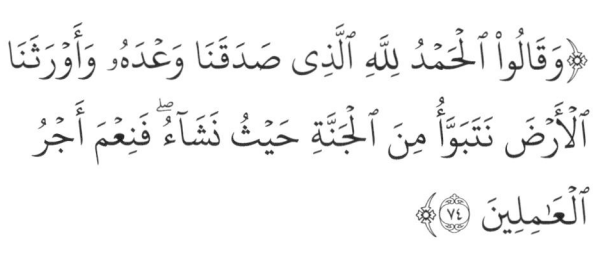

﴿وَقَالُوا۟ ٱلْحَمْدُ لِلَّهِ ٱلَّذِى صَدَقَنَا وَعْدَهُۥ وَأَوْرَثَنَا ٱلْأَرْضَ نَتَبَوَّأُ مِنَ ٱلْجَنَّةِ حَيْثُ نَشَآءُ ۖ فَنِعْمَ أَجْرُ ٱلْعَٰمِلِينَ ۝﴾

TAFSEER (EXPLANATION) OF THE VERSE

As your teacher reads the *Tafseer* of al-Imam as-Sa'dee (may Allah have Mercy on him), follow along carefully and take notes on the following points:

1. What is their situation as they say, **"All praise is due to Allah…"**?

2. Which promise has been fulfilled?

3. What is **"this place"**?

4. What is the meaning of dwelling wherever they want?

5. What work had they done and for how long?

6. What kind of reward do they have and for how long?

7. What are some of the ways we know about the greatness of Paradise?

*THE FOLLOWING HADEETH STUDY IS NOT FROM THE TAFSEER OF AL-IMAM AS-SA'DEE.

On the authority of Ibn 'Umar (may Allah be pleased with him and his father), who said: "The Messenger of Allah (may Allah raise his rank and grant him peace) obligated *Zakaat al-Fitr* as a *saa'* of dates or a *saa'* of barley upon every Muslim, free or captive, male or female, young or old. He ordered that it be given out before the people go out for the prayer."
[Agreed upon]

عَنِ ابْنِ عُمَرَ ـ رَضِيَ اللهُ عَنْهُمَا ـ ، قَالَ: "فَرَضَ رَسُولُ اللهِ ـ صَلَّى اللهُ عَلَيْهِ وَسَلَّمَ ـ زَكَاةَ الفِطْرِ صَاعًا مِنْ تَمْرٍ، أَوْ صَاعًا مِنْ شَعِيرٍ، عَلَى العَبْدِ وَالحُرِّ، وَالذَّكَرِ وَالأُنْثَى، وَالصَّغِيرِ وَالكَبِيرِ مِنَ المُسْلِمِينَ، وَأَمَرَ بِهَا أَنْ تُؤَدَّى قَبْلَ خُرُوجِ النَّاسِ إِلَى الصَّلَاةِ." (مُتَّفَقٌ عَلَيْهِ)

Points to consider from this hadeeth:

LESSON 30

ANGELS SURROUND THE THRONE EXALTING HIS PRAISE

قال تعالى:

TODAY'S VERSE

75. And you shall see the angels encircling the throne, exalting their Lord with praise. Judgments are made between them by the truth, and it is said: 'All praise is due to Allah, the Lord of all things.'

﴿وَتَرَى ٱلْمَلَٰٓئِكَةَ حَآفِّينَ مِنْ حَوْلِ ٱلْعَرْشِ يُسَبِّحُونَ بِحَمْدِ رَبِّهِمْ وَقُضِىَ بَيْنَهُم بِٱلْحَقِّ وَقِيلَ ٱلْحَمْدُ لِلَّهِ رَبِّ ٱلْعَٰلَمِينَ ۝﴾

TAFSEER (EXPLANATION) OF THE VERSE

As your teacher reads the *Tafseer* of al-Imam as-Sa'dee (may Allah have Mercy on him), follow along carefully and take notes on the following points:

1. Who is being addressed as **"you"** in this Verse?

2. What can be understood from the description, **"haaf-feen"** (حافين), around the throne?

   A.

   B.

   C.

   D.

   E.

3. What does their exaltation of Allah include?

4. Between whom are judgments made?

5. What is the meaning of the judgments being made **"by the truth"**?

6. Who says, **"All praise is due to Allah..."** as mentioned at the end of the Verse?

7. For what reason are they praising Allah?

73

8. What kind of praise is this?

تم تفسير سورة الزمر بحمد الله وعونه

This explanation of *Soorah az-Zumar* is now complete, by way of Allah's Aid, and with praise due to Him.

AL-HAMDU LILLAAH

All praise is due to Allah! This completes our study of these 75 beautiful verses of this amazing chapter, *Soorah az-Zumar.* May Allah accept these efforts of ours, as well as our fasting and praying, and may He forgive our sins and admit us into Paradise. Indeed, His Promise is true!

﴿ إِنَّ ٱلَّذِينَ ءَامَنُوا۟ وَعَمِلُوا۟ ٱلصَّٰلِحَٰتِ يَهْدِيهِمْ رَبُّهُم بِإِيمَٰنِهِمْ ۖ تَجْرِى مِن تَحْتِهِمُ ٱلْأَنْهَٰرُ فِى جَنَّٰتِ ٱلنَّعِيمِ ۝ دَعْوَىٰهُمْ فِيهَا سُبْحَٰنَكَ ٱللَّهُمَّ وَتَحِيَّتُهُمْ فِيهَا سَلَٰمٌ ۚ وَءَاخِرُ دَعْوَىٰهُمْ أَنِ ٱلْحَمْدُ لِلَّهِ رَبِّ ٱلْعَٰلَمِينَ ۝ ﴾

سورة يونس

Verily those who have believed and worked righteous deeds, their Lord guides them by their faith. Rivers flow from under them in gardens of joy. Their call therein is: *"Subhaanak Allaahumma"* (Exalted You are, O Allah). And their greeting therein is *salaam* (peace). And the last of their call is: "All praise is due to Allah, Lord of all things."

[10: 9-10]

QUIZ 1

REVIEW OF WEEK 1: LESSONS 1-7 (VERSES 1-16)

QUIZ 1: REVIEW QUESTIONS

The following questions are designed to test your understanding of the first 16 Verses of Soorah az-Zumar and the explanation of al-Imam as-Sa'dee. After taking the quiz on your own, check your answers with the Answer Key on p.98.

1. Which names does al-Imam as-Sa'dee provide for this chapter?
    A. *Soorah az-Zumar* and *Soorah al-Ghuraf*
    B. *Soorah az-Zumar* only
    C. *Soorah az-Zumar, Soorah al-Ghuraf*, and *Soorah Tanzeel*
    D. none of the above

2. How does al-Imam as-Sa'dee classify *Soorah az-Zumar*?
    A. *Makkiyyah*
    B. *Madaniyyah*
    C. He does not classify this *soorah* at all.
    D. Part *Makkiyyah* and part *Madaniyyah*

3. Why did the polytheists take intermediaries between themselves and Allah, as explained by al-Imam as-Sa'dee in his *Tafseer* of Verse 3?
    A. Because they never believed in Allah.
    B. Because one of the prophets told them to do it.
    C. Because they considered Allah to be similar to His creation.
    D. none of the above

4. Complete the meaning of Verse 3: **"Indeed, Allah does not guide one who is: _____."**
    A. a liar, an ingrate
    B. an arrogant boastful person
    C. a disbeliever who follows his desires
    D. a confused person

5. What relationship is understood between the two Names, *al-Waahid* (the Singular One) and *al-Qahhaar* (the Ever Dominating One)?
    A. Each meaning necessitates the other.
    B. Since He is al-Waahid, He cannot be al-Qahhaar at the same time.
    C. These are two Names of Allah; they are also two names of the Prophet ﷺ.
    D. none of the above

6. How does al-Imam as-Sa'dee explain the appointed time set for the sun and the moon, mentioned in Verse 5?

    A. It is the daily setting of each one.
    B. It is the end of this worldly life.
    C. It depends on the climate and length of the day in each country.
    D. It is the end of each lunar month.

7. Does the name, *al-Ghaffaar* (the Oft Forgiving), include the meaning of divine forgiveness for those who commit polytheism?

    A. No, since Allah does not forgive shirk (polytheism).
    B. Yes, in all cases.
    C. Yes, but only if they had sincerely repented.
    D. We have no way of knowing this issue.

8. Which of the following are **NOT** from the eight paired animals mentioned in Verse 6?

    A. sheep
    B. cows
    C. camels
    D. horses

9. How does al-Imam as-Sa'dee explain the meaning of Verse 7, **"Then, unto your Lord is your return, and He informs you of what you had done…"**?

    A. He informs you based on His perfect knowledge.
    B. He informs you based on the writing of the angels.
    C. He causes your own limbs to testify against you.
    D. all of the above

10. According to al-Imam as-Sa'dee, why is the Prophet (may Allah raise his rank and grant him peace) ordered to be the first of the Muslims in Verse 12?

    A. So he would be a Muslim before Ibraaheem or any other prophet.
    B. Because one who leads others should be the first to act by his own teachings.
    C. So he could become the first one to enter Paradise.
    D. all of the above

ANSWER KEY: See p.98.

QUIZ 2

REVIEW OF WEEK 2: LESSONS 8-14 (VERSES 17-35)

QUIZ 2: REVIEW QUESTIONS

The following questions are designed to test your understanding of Verses 17-35 of Soorah az-Zumar and the explanation of al-Imam as-Sa'dee. After taking the quiz on your own, check your answers with the Answer Key on p.98.

1. Which of the following conclusions can be reached from reading the discussion of al-Imam as-Sa'dee on the topic of *tamyeez* (the ability to distinguish between right and wrong) in his explanation of Verse 18?

    A. All who possess *tamyeez* are ultimately successful.
    B. Some of those who possess *tamyeez* are ultimately successful.
    C. *Tamyeez* has nothing to do with success in this life or the Next.
    D. none of the above

2. How does al-Imam as-Sa'dee explain the *"ghuraf"* (rooms) mentioned in Verse 20?

    A. They are lofty, decorated dwellings in Paradise.
    B. They are found under Allah's throne and in al-Firdows (the loftiest heights).
    C. Their carpets are made of gold-embroidered green silk.
    D. all of the above

3. Paired similitudes providing insightful comparisons are found in the Quran:

    A. often
    B. rarely
    C. never
    D. in every Verse

4. How does al-Imam as-Sa'dee explain the warning of *"wayl"* (ويل) in Verse 22?

    A. It is the name of a valley in the Hellfire.
    B. It is the gradual increase of torment in the Hellfire.
    C. It is a pool of pus collected from the wounds of those burning in Hell.
    D. none of the above

5. How does al-Imam as-Sa'dee explain the description of the Quran as *"mutashaabih"* (متشابه), as found in Verse 23?

    A. the historical accuracy of all information in it
    B. the perfect alignment of its meanings without contradictions
    C. ambiguity and potential confusion if it is contemplated too deeply
    D. that it is full of scientific miracles

6. What topics does al-Imam as-Sa'dee say are mentioned in the Quran in paired examples of contrast, in his explanation of the word, *"mathaanee"* (مَثَانِي), in Verse 23?

    A. stories
    B. traits of good and evil people
    C. rulings
    D. all of the above

7. In his explanation of Verse 23, what special insight does al-Imam as-Sa'dee reveal about his methodology of explaining the Quran?

    A. that he wrote his entire Tafseer in less than seven months
    B. he summarized the *Tafseer* of al-Imam al-Baghawee
    C. that his students compiled his *Tafseer* from various books he wrote
    D. he explains each passage in its context, even phrases previously explained

8. Why do disbelievers try to ward off the Hellfire using their faces?

    A. because their hands and feet are shackled
    B. because everything else is already burned off
    C. This is just the decision they make after being given the choice.
    D. because their false advisors told them this would work

9. According to al-Imam as-Sa'dee, what does Verse 30 about the Prophet (may Allah raise his rank and grant him peace) being dead actually mean?

    A. All people will certainly die.
    B. He would die before the end of that year.
    C. His death had already been delayed five times.
    D. none of the above

10. What example of speaking about Allah without knowledge did al-Imam as-Sa'dee provide in his explanation of Verse 32?

    A. claiming to be a prophet
    B. ascribing things to Allah that are not befitting His perfection
    C. claiming He said things that He did not say
    D. all of the above

ANSWER KEY: See p.98.

QUIZ 3

REVIEW OF WEEK 3: LESSONS 15-21 (VERSES 36-59)

QUIZ 3: REVIEW QUESTIONS

The following questions are designed to test your understanding of Verses 36-59 of Soorah az-Zumar and the explanation of al-Imam as-Sa'dee. After taking the quiz on your own, check your answers with the Answer Key on p.98.

1. Complete the meaning of Verse 38: **"And if you asked them: 'Who created the heavens and the earth?' They certainly say: _____."**

    A. Shaytaan
    B. our forefathers of old
    C. Allah
    D. Manaat

2. According to al-Imam as-Sa'dee, who is being ordered to tell the disbelievers to go on doing their deeds as they have been doing them (in Verse 39)?

    A. Muhammad (may Allah raise his rank and grant him peace)
    B. every believer in Allah and the Last Day
    C. Nooh (Noah) (may Allah raise his rank and grant him peace)
    D. Aboo Bakr as-Siddeeq

3. In Verse 41, what does it mean that the Prophet (may Allah raise his rank and grant him peace) was not sent as a **"wakeel"** over the people?

    A. He was not sent to advise them.
    B. He was not sent to be a witness over them.
    C. He was not sent to force them to do things.
    D. all of the above

4. When does Allah take people's souls?

    A. at the time of death
    B. during sleep
    C. both A and B
    D. Only the Angel of Death takes souls; we do not say that Allah takes souls.

5. What is the lesser form of death?

    A. being in a coma
    B. sleep
    C. clinical death before life-saving efforts are attempted
    D. the life of the grave

6. Based on al-Imam as-Sa'dee's explanation of Verse 44 [which means], **"Say: To Allah [alone] belongs all intercession,"** what is true about the issue of intercession in the Hereafter?

    A. All claims that some people can intercede are false.
    B. Some people have permission to intercede; they can do this whenever they wish.
    C. Any person of *towheed* can intercede for another, without any limit.
    D. Intercession, when allowed by Allah, is an honor for the one interceding.

7. What causes the polytheists to rejoice?

    A. when Allah is mentioned alone
    B. when their objects of worship are mentioned
    C. when Verses of the Quran are recited near them
    D. when the military victories of the Muslims are mentioned

8. What usually happens when polytheists call upon Allah in times of distress, and then Allah responds to their call and saves them from their situation? (As mentioned in Verse 49.)

    A. They forget this favor and return back to the worship of others.
    B. They love Allah more and worship Him alone sometimes.
    C. They abandon their false objects of worship.
    D. They doubt their idols' abilities to save them from disasters.

9. In his explanation of Verse 52, al-Imam as-Sa'dee stated that _____ is/are something given to all people, while _____ is/are only given to the best of them.

    A. money, fame and respect
    B. faith, success
    C. sustenance, righteous actions
    D. wealth, children and success

10. In Verse 53, what does al-Imam as-Sa'dee say about the relationship between Allah's Forgiveness and His Mercy?

    A. He is always described with both of them.
    B. Forgiveness is only in this life; Mercy is in the Hereafter.
    C. His Forgiveness is restricted by His Mercy and Sovereignty.
    D. His Anger overtakes both of them on the Day of Judgment.

ANSWER KEY: See p.98.

QUIZ 4

REVIEW OF WEEK 4: LESSONS 22-28 (VERSES 60-73)

QUIZ 4: REVIEW QUESTIONS

The following questions are designed to test your understanding of Verses 60-73 of Soorah az-Zumar and the explanation of al-Imam as-Sa'dee. After taking the quiz on your own, check your answers with the Answer Key on p.98.

1. Who shall have dark faces on the Day of Judgment? (as mentioned in Verse 60)
    A. those who lied on Allah
    B. those who had dark skin color in this world
    C. believers who committed sins
    D. all of the above

2. Since Allah has created all things (as mentioned in Verse 62), this means:
    A. His Attributes are created.
    B. The Quran is created.
    C. You cannot refer to Allah as a "thing"; that would mean He is created.
    D. none of the above

3. According to al-Imam as-Sa'dee, what is the meaning of *"maqaaleed"* used in Verse 63?
    A. keys
    B. blind followers
    C. piety
    D. none of the above

4. Which of the following does al-Imam as-Sa'dee mention as an example of a blessing which Allah must be thanked for, in his explanation of Verse 66?
    A. physical health and well-being
    B. provisions
    C. sincerity and piety
    D. all of the above

5. Complete the meaning of Verse 67: **"The entire earth on the Day of Resurrection shall be _____, and the heavens shall be rolled up in His right Hand."**
    A. in His grasp
    B. destroyed
    C. one flat plain
    D. rolled up

6. What is the name of the angel who blows the horn at the end of the world?

    A. Jibreel
    B. Meekaal
    C. Israafeel
    D. Israa'eel

7. In his explanation of Verse 68, how many times does al-Imam as-Sa'dee say the horn shall be blown?

    A. 1
    B. 2
    C. 3
    D. 4

8. Based on a subtle benefit within the language of the Verses about the people arriving at the gates of Hell and those arriving at the gates of Paradise, which group did al-Imam as-Sa'dee say would arrive at the gates but not enter immediately?

    A. the people of Hell
    B. the people of Paradise
    C. both groups
    D. neither group

9. Complete the meaning of Verse 72: **"It is said: Enter through the gates of Jahannam, abiding therein forever; what a terrible abode that is for the _____."**

    A. disbelievers
    B. polytheists
    C. arrogant
    D. liars

10. Which of the following is true about Paradise and the Hellfire?

    A. Paradise has gates; the Hellfire does not have gates.
    B. They both have caretakers from among the angels.
    C. both A and B
    D. neither A nor B

ANSWER KEY: See p.98.

QUIZ 5

REVIEW OF SOORAH AZ-ZUMAR (VERSES 1-75) & ITS TAFSEER

QUIZ: COMPREHENSIVE REVIEW QUESTIONS

The following questions are designed to test your understanding of Soorah az-Zumar and the explanation of al-Imam as-Sa'dee. After taking the quiz on your own, check your answers with the Answer Key on p.98.

1. Why did the polytheists take intermediaries between themselves and Allah, as explained by al-Imam as-Sa'dee in his *Tafseer* of Verse 3?

    A. Because they truly believed in Allah.
    B. Because it was written in their ancient scriptures.
    C. Because they considered Allah to be similar to His creation.
    D. both B and C

2. What relationship is understood between the two Names, *al-Waahid* (the Singular One) and *al-Qahhaar* (the Ever Dominating One)?

    A. Each meaning necessitates the other.
    B. Since He is al-Waahid, He cannot be al-Qahhaar at the same time.
    C. These are two Names of Allah; they are also two names of the Prophet ﷺ.
    D. all of the above

3. How does al-Imam as-Sa'dee explain the appointed time set for the sun and the moon, mentioned in Verse 5?

    A. It is the end of each solar month.
    B. It is the end of this worldly life.
    C. It depends of the climate and length of the day in each country.
    D. It is the daily setting of the sun.

4. Does the name, *al-Ghaffaar* (the Oft Forgiving), include the meaning of divine forgiveness for those who commit polytheism?

    A. No, since Allah does not forgive shirk (polytheism).
    B. Yes, in all cases.
    C. Yes, but only if they had sincerely repented.
    D. We have no way of knowing this issue.

5. How does al-Imam as-Sa'dee explain the meaning of Verse 7, **"Then, unto your Lord is your return, and He informs you of what you had done..."**?

    A. He informs you based on His perfect and comprehensive knowledge.
    B. He informs you about your deeds based on the writing of the angels.
    C. He brings your own limbs as witnesses against you.
    D. all of the above

6. According to al-Imam as-Sa'dee, why is the Prophet (may Allah raise his rank and grant him peace) ordered to be the first of the Muslims in Verse 12?
    A. So he would be a Muslim before Ibraaheem or any other prophet.
    B. Because one who leads others should be the first to act by his own teachings.
    C. So he could become the first one to enter Paradise.
    D. all of the above

7. According to al-Imam as-Sa'dee, what is true about *tamyeez*, the ability to distinguish between right and wrong (from his explanation of Verse 18)?
    A. All who possess *tamyeez* are ultimately successful.
    B. Some of those who possess *tamyeez* are ultimately successful.
    C. *Tamyeez* has nothing to do with success in this life or the Next.
    D. none of the above

8. How does al-Imam as-Sa'dee explain the *"ghuraf"* (rooms) mentioned in Verse 20?
    A. They are lofty, decorated dwellings in Paradise.
    B. They are found under Allah's throne and in al-Firdows (the loftiest heights).
    C. Their carpets are made of gold-embroidered green silk.
    D. all of the above

9. How does al-Imam as-Sa'dee explain the warning of *"wayl"* (ويل) in Verse 22?
    A. It is the name of a valley in the Hellfire.
    B. It is the gradual increase of torment in the Hellfire.
    C. It is a pool of pus collected from the wounds of those burning in Hell.
    D. none of the above

10. How does al-Imam as-Sa'dee explain the description of the Quran as *"mutashaabih"* (متشابه), as found in Verse 23?
    A. The historical accuracy of all information in it is confirmed by all nations.
    B. the perfect alignment of its meanings without contradictions
    C. ambiguity and potential confusion if it is contemplated too deeply
    D. that it is full of scientific miracles

11. What topics does al-Imam as-Sa'dee say are mentioned in the Quran in paired examples of contrast, explaining the word, *"mathaanee"* (مثاني), in Verse 23?
    A. stories
    B. traits of good and evil people
    C. rulings
    D. all of the above

12. Why do disbelievers try to ward off the Hellfire using their faces?
    A. because their hands and feet are shackled
    B. because everything else is already burned off
    C. This is just the decision they make after being given the choice.
    D. because their false advisors told them this would work

13. What example of speaking about Allah without knowledge does al-Imam as-Sa'dee provide in his explanation of Verse 32?

    A. claiming to be a prophet
    B. ascribing things to Allah that are not befitting His perfection
    C. claiming He said things that He did not say
    D. all of the above

14. Complete the meaning of Verse 38: **"And if you asked them: 'Who created the heavens and the earth?' They certainly say: _____."**

    A. Allah
    B. our main three idols
    C. 'Abdul-Muttalib
    D. Manaat exclusively

15. In Verse 41, what does it mean that the Prophet (may Allah raise his rank and grant him peace) was not sent as a *"wakeel"* over the people?

    A. He was not sent to advise them or correct their behavior.
    B. He was not sent to be a witness over them.
    C. He was not sent to force them to do things.
    D. none of the above

16. What is the lesser form of death?

    A. little or no brain activity
    B. a confirmed medical death
    C. the life of the grave
    D. none of the above

17. Based on al-Imam as-Sa'dee's explanation of Verse 44 (which means), **"Say: To Allah [alone] belongs all intercession,"** what is true about intercession in the Hereafter?

    A. All claims that people can intercede are rejected.
    B. Some people have permission to intercede; they can do this whenever they wish.
    C. Any person of *towheed* can intercede for another, without any limit.
    D. Intercession, when allowed by Allah, is a show of mercy for those interceded for.

18. In his explanation of Verse 52, al-Imam as-Sa'dee stated that _____ is/are something given to all people, while _____ is/are only given to the best of them.

    A. sustenance, righteous actions
    B. faith, success
    C. money, fame
    D. wealth, children and success

19. In Verse 53, what does al-Imam as-Sa'dee say about the relationship between Allah's Forgiveness and His Mercy?

    A. They come together and are inseparable.
    B. Mercy is only in this life; Forgiveness is in the Hereafter.
    C. His Mercy is restricted by His Power and Sovereignty.
    D. His Anger overtakes both of them on the Day of Judgment.

20. Which of the following does al-Imam as-Sa'dee mention as an example of a blessing which Allah must be thanked for, in his explanation of Verse 66?

    A. physical health and well-being
    B. provisions
    C. sincerity and piety
    D. all of the above

21. Complete the meaning of Verse 67: **"The entire earth on the Day of Resurrection shall be in His grasp, and the heavens shall be _____."**

    A. in His grasp as well
    B. annihilated
    C. turned into dust
    D. rolled up in His right hand

22. What is the name of the angel who blows the horn at the end of the world?

    A. Jibraa'eel
    B. Meekaa'eel
    C. Israa'eel
    D. Israafeel

23. Based on a subtle benefit within the language of the Verses about the people arriving at the gates of Hell and those arriving at the gates of Paradise, which group did al-Imam as-Sa'dee say would arrive at the gates and enter without any delay?

    A. the people of Hell
    B. the people of Paradise
    C. both groups
    D. neither group

24. Which place is being referred to in Verse 74, **"...The One who kept his promise and made us to inherit this place"**?

    A. the entire earth in this worldly life
    B. Palestine
    C. Makkah
    D. Paradise

25. Regarding the meaning of Verse 75, **"Judgments are made between them by the truth, and it is said: 'All praise is due to Allah…"** whom did al-Imam as-Sa'dee say **"between them"** refers to?

    A. the first and last of the entire creation
    B. the angels and the prophets
    C. the angels
    D. humans and jinn

ANSWER KEY: See p.98.

APPENDIX I: SOORAH AZ-ZUMAR
AND A TRANSLATION OF ITS MEANINGS

In the Name of Allah, the Most Gracious, the Ever Merciful

بِسْمِ ٱللَّهِ ٱلرَّحْمَٰنِ ٱلرَّحِيمِ

1. [This is] Revelation of the Book from Allah, the Almighty, the Ever Wise and Authoritative.

تَنزِيلُ ٱلْكِتَٰبِ مِنَ ٱللَّهِ ٱلْعَزِيزِ ٱلْحَكِيمِ ۝

2. Verily, We have sent down the Book to you, in truth, so worship Allah, as a sincere servant, making the [entire] Religion for Him [alone].

إِنَّآ أَنزَلْنَآ إِلَيْكَ ٱلْكِتَٰبَ بِٱلْحَقِّ فَٱعْبُدِ ٱللَّهَ مُخْلِصًا لَّهُ ٱلدِّينَ ۝

3. Nay! Due to Allah [alone] is [all] sincere religiosity. Those who take protectors other than Him [say]: 'We only worship them to draw near to Allah, with more closeness.' Indeed, Allah shall judge between them about what they differ over. Indeed, Allah does not guide one who is a liar, an ingrate.

أَلَا لِلَّهِ ٱلدِّينُ ٱلْخَالِصُ وَٱلَّذِينَ ٱتَّخَذُوا۟ مِن دُونِهِۦٓ أَوْلِيَآءَ مَا نَعْبُدُهُمْ إِلَّا لِيُقَرِّبُونَآ إِلَى ٱللَّهِ زُلْفَىٰٓ إِنَّ ٱللَّهَ يَحْكُمُ بَيْنَهُمْ فِى مَا هُمْ فِيهِ يَخْتَلِفُونَ إِنَّ ٱللَّهَ لَا يَهْدِى مَنْ هُوَ كَٰذِبٌ كَفَّارٌ ۝

4. Had Allah wanted to have a son, He would have selected whomever He willed from those He has created; exalted He is! He is Allah, the Uniquely Singular One, the Ever Dominating One.

لَّوْ أَرَادَ ٱللَّهُ أَن يَتَّخِذَ وَلَدًا لَّٱصْطَفَىٰ مِمَّا يَخْلُقُ مَا يَشَآءُ سُبْحَٰنَهُۥ هُوَ ٱللَّهُ ٱلْوَٰحِدُ ٱلْقَهَّارُ ۝

5. He created the heavens and the earth, in truth. He makes the night merge into the day, and He makes the day merge into the night. He has made the sun and the moon to be of service [to mankind's needs]. Each runs [its course] until a set time. Nay! He is the Almighty, the Oft-Forgiving.

خَلَقَ ٱلسَّمَٰوَٰتِ وَٱلْأَرْضَ بِٱلْحَقِّ يُكَوِّرُ ٱلَّيْلَ عَلَى ٱلنَّهَارِ وَيُكَوِّرُ ٱلنَّهَارَ عَلَى ٱلَّيْلِ وَسَخَّرَ ٱلشَّمْسَ وَٱلْقَمَرَ كُلٌّ يَجْرِى لِأَجَلٍ مُّسَمًّى أَلَا هُوَ ٱلْعَزِيزُ ٱلْغَفَّٰرُ ۝

6. He created you [all] from a single soul, and then He made for it its mate. He sent down for you eight kinds of cattle in pairs. He creates you in the wombs of your mothers, in stage after stage of formation, under three levels of darkness. Such is Allah, your Lord, to Him belongs the [entire] dominion. No one deserves worship other than Him, so how can you be turned away?

خَلَقَكُم مِّن نَّفْسٍ وَٰحِدَةٍ ثُمَّ جَعَلَ مِنْهَا زَوْجَهَا وَأَنزَلَ لَكُم مِّنَ ٱلْأَنْعَٰمِ ثَمَٰنِيَةَ أَزْوَٰجٍ يَخْلُقُكُمْ فِى بُطُونِ أُمَّهَٰتِكُمْ خَلْقًا مِّنۢ بَعْدِ خَلْقٍ فِى ظُلُمَٰتٍ ثَلَٰثٍ ذَٰلِكُمُ ٱللَّهُ رَبُّكُمْ لَهُ ٱلْمُلْكُ لَآ إِلَٰهَ إِلَّا هُوَ فَأَنَّىٰ تُصْرَفُونَ ۝

7. If you [all] disbelieve, Allah certainly remains without any need [for you]. He is not pleased with disbelief for His worshippers. If you are grateful, He is pleased with that for you. No one shall bear the burden of another. Then, unto your Lord is your return, and He informs you of what you had done. Indeed, He is All-Knowing about the realities of [people's] chests.

8. Whenever a harm reaches a person, he calls upon his Lord [alone], in repentance to Him. Then, when He returns His favor [of safety] back to him, he forgets what he supplicated about previously and sets up partners with Allah, in order to lead [himself and others] away from His Path. Say: 'Enjoy your disbelief for a moment; you will indeed be from the dwellers of the Fire.'

9. Otherwise, what about someone devoutly obedient, in prostration at times at night and standing, worried about the Hereafter, hoping for the Mercy of his Lord? Say: 'Are those who know equal to those who do not know?' It is only the people of intellect who take admonition.

10. Say: 'O My worshippers who have believed, be pious unto Allah. Those who are piously proficient in this life shall have goodness. Allah's earth is spacious. It is only the patient ones who shall receive their reward without measure.'

11. Say: 'I have certainly been ordered to worship Allah, making the religion sincerely and purely for Him [alone].'

12. 'And I have been commanded to be the first of the Muslims.'

13. Say: 'I do indeed fear the punishment of a tremendous day, if I were to disobey my Lord.'

إِن تَكْفُرُوا۟ فَإِنَّ ٱللَّهَ غَنِىٌّ عَنكُمْ ۖ وَلَا يَرْضَىٰ لِعِبَادِهِ ٱلْكُفْرَ ۖ وَإِن تَشْكُرُوا۟ يَرْضَهُ لَكُمْ ۗ وَلَا تَزِرُ وَازِرَةٌ وِزْرَ أُخْرَىٰ ۗ ثُمَّ إِلَىٰ رَبِّكُم مَّرْجِعُكُمْ فَيُنَبِّئُكُم بِمَا كُنتُمْ تَعْمَلُونَ ۚ إِنَّهُۥ عَلِيمٌۢ بِذَاتِ ٱلصُّدُورِ ۝

وَإِذَا مَسَّ ٱلْإِنسَـٰنَ ضُرٌّ دَعَا رَبَّهُۥ مُنِيبًا إِلَيْهِ ثُمَّ إِذَا خَوَّلَهُۥ نِعْمَةً مِّنْهُ نَسِىَ مَا كَانَ يَدْعُوٓا۟ إِلَيْهِ مِن قَبْلُ وَجَعَلَ لِلَّهِ أَندَادًا لِّيُضِلَّ عَن سَبِيلِهِۦ ۚ قُلْ تَمَتَّعْ بِكُفْرِكَ قَلِيلًا ۖ إِنَّكَ مِنْ أَصْحَـٰبِ ٱلنَّارِ ۝

أَمَّنْ هُوَ قَـٰنِتٌ ءَانَآءَ ٱلَّيْلِ سَاجِدًا وَقَآئِمًا يَحْذَرُ ٱلْـَٔاخِرَةَ وَيَرْجُوا۟ رَحْمَةَ رَبِّهِۦ ۗ قُلْ هَلْ يَسْتَوِى ٱلَّذِينَ يَعْلَمُونَ وَٱلَّذِينَ لَا يَعْلَمُونَ ۗ إِنَّمَا يَتَذَكَّرُ أُو۟لُوا۟ ٱلْأَلْبَـٰبِ ۝

قُلْ يَـٰعِبَادِ ٱلَّذِينَ ءَامَنُوا۟ ٱتَّقُوا۟ رَبَّكُمْ ۚ لِلَّذِينَ أَحْسَنُوا۟ فِى هَـٰذِهِ ٱلدُّنْيَا حَسَنَةٌ ۗ وَأَرْضُ ٱللَّهِ وَٰسِعَةٌ ۗ إِنَّمَا يُوَفَّى ٱلصَّـٰبِرُونَ أَجْرَهُم بِغَيْرِ حِسَابٍ ۝

قُلْ إِنِّىٓ أُمِرْتُ أَنْ أَعْبُدَ ٱللَّهَ مُخْلِصًا لَّهُ ٱلدِّينَ ۝

وَأُمِرْتُ لِأَنْ أَكُونَ أَوَّلَ ٱلْمُسْلِمِينَ ۝

قُلْ إِنِّىٓ أَخَافُ إِنْ عَصَيْتُ رَبِّى عَذَابَ يَوْمٍ عَظِيمٍ ۝

14. Say: 'Allah is who I worship, making my religion purely and sincerely for Him [alone].'

15. 'So worship whatever you want less than Him.' Say: 'Indeed, the losers are those who lose themselves and their families on the Day of Resurrection. Nay! Such is the [most] evident loss!'

16. They shall have coverings of Fire from above them, and coverings from below them as well. Such is how Allah strikes fear in His worshippers. O My worshippers! Be pious unto Me!

17. Those who shun the worship of false deities and turn to Allah in repentance shall have glad tidings, so proclaim glad tidings to My worshippers!

18. It is those who listen to the word and then follow the best of it who are the ones Allah has guided; it is they who are people of intellect.

19. Yet the one upon whom the verdict of punishment rightfully applies, are you going to save him from the Fire?

20. But those who are pious unto their Lord shall have rooms, with rooms built above them, as rivers flow underneath them. A promise from Allah; Allah does not break His promise of reward.

21. Have you not seen that Allah sends down water from the sky, and then causes it to take paths down into the ground? Then, He brings forth from it vegetation of various colors. Then, it withers, and you see it turn yellow, and then He makes it become straw. Indeed, there is a reminder in that for people of intellect.

قُلِ ٱللَّهَ أَعْبُدُ مُخْلِصًا لَّهُ دِينِى ۝

فَٱعْبُدُواْ مَا شِئْتُم مِّن دُونِهِۦ ۗ قُلْ إِنَّ ٱلْخَـٰسِرِينَ ٱلَّذِينَ خَسِرُوٓاْ أَنفُسَهُمْ وَأَهْلِيهِمْ يَوْمَ ٱلْقِيَـٰمَةِ ۗ أَلَا ذَٰلِكَ هُوَ ٱلْخُسْرَانُ ٱلْمُبِينُ ۝

لَهُم مِّن فَوْقِهِمْ ظُلَلٌ مِّنَ ٱلنَّارِ وَمِن تَحْتِهِمْ ظُلَلٌ ۚ ذَٰلِكَ يُخَوِّفُ ٱللَّهُ بِهِۦ عِبَادَهُۥ ۚ يَـٰعِبَادِ فَٱتَّقُونِ ۝

وَٱلَّذِينَ ٱجْتَنَبُواْ ٱلطَّـٰغُوتَ أَن يَعْبُدُوهَا وَأَنَابُوٓاْ إِلَى ٱللَّهِ لَهُمُ ٱلْبُشْرَىٰ ۚ فَبَشِّرْ عِبَادِ ۝

ٱلَّذِينَ يَسْتَمِعُونَ ٱلْقَوْلَ فَيَتَّبِعُونَ أَحْسَنَهُۥٓ ۚ أُوْلَـٰٓئِكَ ٱلَّذِينَ هَدَىٰهُمُ ٱللَّهُ ۖ وَأُوْلَـٰٓئِكَ هُمْ أُوْلُواْ ٱلْأَلْبَـٰبِ ۝

أَفَمَنْ حَقَّ عَلَيْهِ كَلِمَةُ ٱلْعَذَابِ أَفَأَنتَ تُنقِذُ مَن فِى ٱلنَّارِ ۝

لَـٰكِنِ ٱلَّذِينَ ٱتَّقَوْاْ رَبَّهُمْ لَهُمْ غُرَفٌ مِّن فَوْقِهَا غُرَفٌ مَّبْنِيَّةٌ تَجْرِى مِن تَحْتِهَا ٱلْأَنْهَـٰرُ ۖ وَعْدَ ٱللَّهِ ۖ لَا يُخْلِفُ ٱللَّهُ ٱلْمِيعَادَ ۝

أَلَمْ تَرَ أَنَّ ٱللَّهَ أَنزَلَ مِنَ ٱلسَّمَآءِ مَآءً فَسَلَكَهُۥ يَنَـٰبِيعَ فِى ٱلْأَرْضِ ثُمَّ يُخْرِجُ بِهِۦ زَرْعًا مُّخْتَلِفًا أَلْوَٰنُهُۥ ثُمَّ يَهِيجُ فَتَرَىٰهُ مُصْفَرًّا ثُمَّ يَجْعَلُهُۥ حُطَـٰمًا ۚ إِنَّ فِى ذَٰلِكَ لَذِكْرَىٰ لِأُوْلِى ٱلْأَلْبَـٰبِ ۝

22. Or [consider] the one whom Allah expands his breast to accept Islam, and so he is upon a light from his Lord. So then woe to those whose hearts have hardened from the remembrance of Allah! Such are in manifest misguidance.

23. Allah has sent down the finest discourse, a familiar Book with parables of contrast, causing the skins of those who fear their Lord to shiver, and their skins and their hearts then soften to the remembrance of Allah. Such is the guidance of Allah; He guides whomsoever He wills. And whomever Allah sends astray shall have no one to guide him.

24. Or [consider] the one who tries to ward off the punishment with his face on the Day of Resurrection! It shall be said to the oppressive ones: 'Taste what you have earned!'

25. Those before them had also disbelieved, and so the punishment came to them from where they could not even perceive.

26. So Allah made them taste the disgrace in this worldly life, and the punishment of the Hereafter is even greater, if they only knew!

27. We have put forth every type of parable for people in this Quran, so they could heed the reminder.

28. An Arabic Quran, having no crookedness, so they could become pious.

29. Allah has provided the parable of a slave belonging to multiple owners in disagreement and another belonging to a single owner. Are they equal in comparison? All praise is due to Allah, yet most of them do not know.

30. Indeed, you are dead, and they are also certainly all dead.

أَفَمَن شَرَحَ ٱللَّهُ صَدْرَهُۥ لِلْإِسْلَٰمِ فَهُوَ عَلَىٰ نُورٍ مِّن رَّبِّهِۦ ۚ فَوَيْلٌ لِّلْقَٰسِيَةِ قُلُوبُهُم مِّن ذِكْرِ ٱللَّهِ ۚ أُو۟لَٰٓئِكَ فِى ضَلَٰلٍ مُّبِينٍ ۝

ٱللَّهُ نَزَّلَ أَحْسَنَ ٱلْحَدِيثِ كِتَٰبًا مُّتَشَٰبِهًا مَّثَانِىَ تَقْشَعِرُّ مِنْهُ جُلُودُ ٱلَّذِينَ يَخْشَوْنَ رَبَّهُمْ ثُمَّ تَلِينُ جُلُودُهُمْ وَقُلُوبُهُمْ إِلَىٰ ذِكْرِ ٱللَّهِ ۚ ذَٰلِكَ هُدَى ٱللَّهِ يَهْدِى بِهِۦ مَن يَشَآءُ ۚ وَمَن يُضْلِلِ ٱللَّهُ فَمَا لَهُۥ مِنْ هَادٍ ۝

أَفَمَن يَتَّقِى بِوَجْهِهِۦ سُوٓءَ ٱلْعَذَابِ يَوْمَ ٱلْقِيَٰمَةِ ۚ وَقِيلَ لِلظَّٰلِمِينَ ذُوقُوا۟ مَا كُنتُمْ تَكْسِبُونَ ۝

كَذَّبَ ٱلَّذِينَ مِن قَبْلِهِمْ فَأَتَىٰهُمُ ٱلْعَذَابُ مِنْ حَيْثُ لَا يَشْعُرُونَ ۝

فَأَذَاقَهُمُ ٱللَّهُ ٱلْخِزْىَ فِى ٱلْحَيَوٰةِ ٱلدُّنْيَا ۖ وَلَعَذَابُ ٱلْءَاخِرَةِ أَكْبَرُ ۚ لَوْ كَانُوا۟ يَعْلَمُونَ ۝

وَلَقَدْ ضَرَبْنَا لِلنَّاسِ فِى هَٰذَا ٱلْقُرْءَانِ مِن كُلِّ مَثَلٍ لَّعَلَّهُمْ يَتَذَكَّرُونَ ۝

قُرْءَانًا عَرَبِيًّا غَيْرَ ذِى عِوَجٍ لَّعَلَّهُمْ يَتَّقُونَ ۝

ضَرَبَ ٱللَّهُ مَثَلًا رَّجُلًا فِيهِ شُرَكَآءُ مُتَشَٰكِسُونَ وَرَجُلًا سَلَمًا لِّرَجُلٍ هَلْ يَسْتَوِيَانِ مَثَلًا ۚ ٱلْحَمْدُ لِلَّهِ ۚ بَلْ أَكْثَرُهُمْ لَا يَعْلَمُونَ ۝

إِنَّكَ مَيِّتٌ وَإِنَّهُم مَّيِّتُونَ ۝

31. Then, on the Day of Resurrection, you will all certainly be in the presence of your Lord, disputing with one another.

32. Who is more oppressive than one who lies upon Allah and rejects the honest truth when it comes to him? Is not Jahannam a suitable abode for the disbelievers?

33. And the one who comes with the honest truth and believes in it [himself], such are the pious ones.

34. They shall have whatever they wish for with their Lord; such is the recompense of the proficiently pious.

35. So that Allah would expiate for them the worst of what they did and reward them based on the best of what they had done.

36. Is not Allah sufficient for His worshipper? And yet they [try to] scare you with those less than Him! Whomever Allah sends astray shall have no one to guide him.

37. Whomever Allah guides shall have no one to lead him astray. Isn't Allah One who is Almighty, the Owner of [just] Retribution?

38. And if you asked them: 'Who created the heavens and the earth?' They certainly say, 'Allah.' Say: 'Do you ever consider those you call upon besides Allah? If Allah decreed some harm to happen to me, could they remove His [decreed] harm? Or if He decreed some Mercy for me, could they withhold His Mercy?!' Say: 'Sufficient for me is Allah! In Him [alone] all those who rely [on someone] must place their trust.'

ثُمَّ إِنَّكُمْ يَوْمَ ٱلْقِيَـٰمَةِ عِندَ رَبِّكُمْ تَخْتَصِمُونَ ﴿٣١﴾

فَمَنْ أَظْلَمُ مِمَّن كَذَبَ عَلَى ٱللَّهِ وَكَذَّبَ بِٱلصِّدْقِ إِذْ جَآءَهُۥٓ ۚ أَلَيْسَ فِى جَهَنَّمَ مَثْوًى لِّلْكَـٰفِرِينَ ﴿٣٢﴾

وَٱلَّذِى جَآءَ بِٱلصِّدْقِ وَصَدَّقَ بِهِۦٓ ۙ أُو۟لَـٰٓئِكَ هُمُ ٱلْمُتَّقُونَ ﴿٣٣﴾

لَهُم مَّا يَشَآءُونَ عِندَ رَبِّهِمْ ۚ ذَٰلِكَ جَزَآءُ ٱلْمُحْسِنِينَ ﴿٣٤﴾

لِيُكَفِّرَ ٱللَّهُ عَنْهُمْ أَسْوَأَ ٱلَّذِى عَمِلُوا۟ وَيَجْزِيَهُمْ أَجْرَهُم بِأَحْسَنِ ٱلَّذِى كَانُوا۟ يَعْمَلُونَ ﴿٣٥﴾

أَلَيْسَ ٱللَّهُ بِكَافٍ عَبْدَهُۥ ۖ وَيُخَوِّفُونَكَ بِٱلَّذِينَ مِن دُونِهِۦ ۚ وَمَن يُضْلِلِ ٱللَّهُ فَمَا لَهُۥ مِنْ هَادٍ ﴿٣٦﴾

وَمَن يَهْدِ ٱللَّهُ فَمَا لَهُۥ مِن مُّضِلٍّ ۗ أَلَيْسَ ٱللَّهُ بِعَزِيزٍ ذِى ٱنتِقَامٍ ﴿٣٧﴾

وَلَئِن سَأَلْتَهُم مَّنْ خَلَقَ ٱلسَّمَـٰوَٰتِ وَٱلْأَرْضَ لَيَقُولُنَّ ٱللَّهُ ۚ قُلْ أَفَرَءَيْتُم مَّا تَدْعُونَ مِن دُونِ ٱللَّهِ إِنْ أَرَادَنِىَ ٱللَّهُ بِضُرٍّ هَلْ هُنَّ كَـٰشِفَـٰتُ ضُرِّهِۦٓ أَوْ أَرَادَنِى بِرَحْمَةٍ هَلْ هُنَّ مُمْسِكَـٰتُ رَحْمَتِهِۦ ۚ قُلْ حَسْبِىَ ٱللَّهُ ۖ عَلَيْهِ يَتَوَكَّلُ ٱلْمُتَوَكِّلُونَ ﴿٣٨﴾

39. Say: 'O my people! Perform your deeds as you do; I also perform deeds. Soon you shall come to know.'

40. 'The one whom punishment comes to, disgracing him, a never-ending punishment covers him.'

41. Indeed, we have sent down to you the Book, for mankind, in truth. Whoever embraces guidance, that is for his own soul. Whoever strays only strays into harm against himself. And you are not a keeper in charge of them!

42. Allah takes the souls at the time of their death, and [the souls of] those who have not [yet] died, while they sleep. He keeps the one He has decreed death for and releases the other, until a set time. Indeed, in that are signs for a people who reflect.

43. Or have they taken those less than Allah as intercessors? Say: 'What if they do not possess any ability, nor have any intellect at all?'

44. Say: 'To Allah [alone] belongs all intercession. To Him belong the dominion of the heavens and the earth, and then back to Him you shall all be returned.'

45. When Allah alone is mentioned, the hearts of those who do not believe in the Hereafter are disgusted, yet when those less than Him are mentioned, they suddenly rejoice!

46. Say: 'O Allah! Creator of the heavens and earth, Knower of [both] the world of the unseen and that of observable affairs, You judge between Your worshippers in all that they have differed over.'

قُلْ يَـٰقَوْمِ ٱعْمَلُوا۟ عَلَىٰ مَكَانَتِكُمْ إِنِّى عَـٰمِلٌ ۖ فَسَوْفَ تَعْلَمُونَ ۝

مَن يَأْتِيهِ عَذَابٌ يُخْزِيهِ وَيَحِلُّ عَلَيْهِ عَذَابٌ مُّقِيمٌ ۝

إِنَّآ أَنزَلْنَا عَلَيْكَ ٱلْكِتَـٰبَ لِلنَّاسِ بِٱلْحَقِّ ۖ فَمَنِ ٱهْتَدَىٰ فَلِنَفْسِهِۦ ۖ وَمَن ضَلَّ فَإِنَّمَا يَضِلُّ عَلَيْهَا ۖ وَمَآ أَنتَ عَلَيْهِم بِوَكِيلٍ ۝

ٱللَّهُ يَتَوَفَّى ٱلْأَنفُسَ حِينَ مَوْتِهَا وَٱلَّتِى لَمْ تَمُتْ فِى مَنَامِهَا ۖ فَيُمْسِكُ ٱلَّتِى قَضَىٰ عَلَيْهَا ٱلْمَوْتَ وَيُرْسِلُ ٱلْأُخْرَىٰٓ إِلَىٰٓ أَجَلٍ مُّسَمًّى ۚ إِنَّ فِى ذَٰلِكَ لَـَٔايَـٰتٍ لِّقَوْمٍ يَتَفَكَّرُونَ ۝

أَمِ ٱتَّخَذُوا۟ مِن دُونِ ٱللَّهِ شُفَعَآءَ ۚ قُلْ أَوَلَوْ كَانُوا۟ لَا يَمْلِكُونَ شَيْـًٔا وَلَا يَعْقِلُونَ ۝

قُل لِّلَّهِ ٱلشَّفَـٰعَةُ جَمِيعًا ۖ لَّهُۥ مُلْكُ ٱلسَّمَـٰوَٰتِ وَٱلْأَرْضِ ۖ ثُمَّ إِلَيْهِ تُرْجَعُونَ ۝

وَإِذَا ذُكِرَ ٱللَّهُ وَحْدَهُ ٱشْمَأَزَّتْ قُلُوبُ ٱلَّذِينَ لَا يُؤْمِنُونَ بِٱلْـَٔاخِرَةِ ۖ وَإِذَا ذُكِرَ ٱلَّذِينَ مِن دُونِهِۦٓ إِذَا هُمْ يَسْتَبْشِرُونَ ۝

قُلِ ٱللَّهُمَّ فَاطِرَ ٱلسَّمَـٰوَٰتِ وَٱلْأَرْضِ عَـٰلِمَ ٱلْغَيْبِ وَٱلشَّهَـٰدَةِ أَنتَ تَحْكُمُ بَيْنَ عِبَادِكَ فِى مَا كَانُوا۟ فِيهِ يَخْتَلِفُونَ ۝

47. Had those who committed injustices owned all that is on earth in its entirety, and another [earth] similar to it, they would certainly offer that as ransom from the terrible punishment of the Day of Resurrection. And what Allah has for them becomes clear to them, what they had not been considering.

48. And the evils of what they earned become clear to them, as what they used to ridicule surrounds them.

49. When harm reaches a person, he calls out to Us, yet later after We deliver him back to Our blessings, he says: 'I was only given this because of knowledge.' Rather, it is a trial, yet most of them do not know.

50. Indeed, this was already said by those before them. Yet, all that they had earned would not suffice them.

51. So the evils of what they earned befell them. And those who committed injustice from among them shall have the evils of what they earn befall them, too, and they shall not escape.

52. Do they not know that Allah extends the provisions for whomsoever He wills and lessens it [for others]. Indeed, there are signs in that for people who believe.

53. Say: 'O My worshippers who have wronged their own souls! Do not give up hope in the Mercy of Allah! Indeed, Allah forgives all sins; it is He who is Ever Forgiving, Ever Merciful.'

54. Repent to your Lord and surrender unto Him before the punishment comes to you, and then you would not be aided.

وَلَوْ أَنَّ لِلَّذِينَ ظَلَمُوا۟ مَا فِى ٱلْأَرْضِ جَمِيعًا وَمِثْلَهُۥ مَعَهُۥ لَٱفْتَدَوْا۟ بِهِۦ مِن سُوٓءِ ٱلْعَذَابِ يَوْمَ ٱلْقِيَٰمَةِ وَبَدَا لَهُم مِّنَ ٱللَّهِ مَا لَمْ يَكُونُوا۟ يَحْتَسِبُونَ ﴿٤٧﴾

وَبَدَا لَهُمْ سَيِّـَٔاتُ مَا كَسَبُوا۟ وَحَاقَ بِهِم مَّا كَانُوا۟ بِهِۦ يَسْتَهْزِءُونَ ﴿٤٨﴾

فَإِذَا مَسَّ ٱلْإِنسَٰنَ ضُرٌّ دَعَانَا ثُمَّ إِذَا خَوَّلْنَٰهُ نِعْمَةً مِّنَّا قَالَ إِنَّمَآ أُوتِيتُهُۥ عَلَىٰ عِلْمٍۭ بَلْ هِىَ فِتْنَةٌ وَلَٰكِنَّ أَكْثَرَهُمْ لَا يَعْلَمُونَ ﴿٤٩﴾

قَدْ قَالَهَا ٱلَّذِينَ مِن قَبْلِهِمْ فَمَآ أَغْنَىٰ عَنْهُم مَّا كَانُوا۟ يَكْسِبُونَ ﴿٥٠﴾

فَأَصَابَهُمْ سَيِّـَٔاتُ مَا كَسَبُوا۟ وَٱلَّذِينَ ظَلَمُوا۟ مِنْ هَٰٓؤُلَآءِ سَيُصِيبُهُمْ سَيِّـَٔاتُ مَا كَسَبُوا۟ وَمَا هُم بِمُعْجِزِينَ ﴿٥١﴾

أَوَلَمْ يَعْلَمُوٓا۟ أَنَّ ٱللَّهَ يَبْسُطُ ٱلرِّزْقَ لِمَن يَشَآءُ وَيَقْدِرُ إِنَّ فِى ذَٰلِكَ لَءَايَٰتٍ لِّقَوْمٍ يُؤْمِنُونَ ﴿٥٢﴾

قُلْ يَٰعِبَادِىَ ٱلَّذِينَ أَسْرَفُوا۟ عَلَىٰٓ أَنفُسِهِمْ لَا تَقْنَطُوا۟ مِن رَّحْمَةِ ٱللَّهِ إِنَّ ٱللَّهَ يَغْفِرُ ٱلذُّنُوبَ جَمِيعًا إِنَّهُۥ هُوَ ٱلْغَفُورُ ٱلرَّحِيمُ ﴿٥٣﴾

وَأَنِيبُوٓا۟ إِلَىٰ رَبِّكُمْ وَأَسْلِمُوا۟ لَهُۥ مِن قَبْلِ أَن يَأْتِيَكُمُ ٱلْعَذَابُ ثُمَّ لَا تُنصَرُونَ ﴿٥٤﴾

55. And follow the best of what was sent down to you from your Lord, before the punishment comes to you suddenly when you do not expect it.

وَٱتَّبِعُوٓا۟ أَحْسَنَ مَآ أُنزِلَ إِلَيْكُم مِّن رَّبِّكُم مِّن قَبْلِ أَن يَأْتِيَكُمُ ٱلْعَذَابُ بَغْتَةً وَأَنتُمْ لَا تَشْعُرُونَ ﴿٥٥﴾

56. Lest a person say: 'What a loss, that I have neglected matters regarding Allah; indeed I had been among those who mocked [the truth].'

أَن تَقُولَ نَفْسٌ يَـٰحَسْرَتَىٰ عَلَىٰ مَا فَرَّطتُ فِى جَنۢبِ ٱللَّهِ وَإِن كُنتُ لَمِنَ ٱلسَّـٰخِرِينَ ﴿٥٦﴾

57. Or lest one say: 'Had Allah only guided me, I would have been among the pious.'

أَوْ تَقُولَ لَوْ أَنَّ ٱللَّهَ هَدَىٰنِى لَكُنتُ مِنَ ٱلْمُتَّقِينَ ﴿٥٧﴾

58. Or lest one say when he sees the punishment: 'If I only had another chance, I would be among the proficiently pious.'

أَوْ تَقُولَ حِينَ تَرَى ٱلْعَذَابَ لَوْ أَنَّ لِى كَرَّةً فَأَكُونَ مِنَ ٱلْمُحْسِنِينَ ﴿٥٨﴾

59. Nay! Our Verses did indeed come to you, yet you disbelieved in them, behaved with arrogance, and became one of the disbelievers!

بَلَىٰ قَدْ جَآءَتْكَ ءَايَـٰتِى فَكَذَّبْتَ بِهَا وَٱسْتَكْبَرْتَ وَكُنتَ مِنَ ٱلْكَـٰفِرِينَ ﴿٥٩﴾

60. On the Day of Resurrection you will see those who lied on Allah, their faces will be darkened. Is not Jahannam the [suitable] abode of the arrogant?

وَيَوْمَ ٱلْقِيَـٰمَةِ تَرَى ٱلَّذِينَ كَذَبُوا۟ عَلَى ٱللَّهِ وُجُوهُهُم مُّسْوَدَّةٌ أَلَيْسَ فِى جَهَنَّمَ مَثْوًى لِّلْمُتَكَبِّرِينَ ﴿٦٠﴾

61. Yet, Allah saves those who were pious, since they had taken the means of salvation; no harm touches them, nor do they grieve.

وَيُنَجِّى ٱللَّهُ ٱلَّذِينَ ٱتَّقَوْا۟ بِمَفَازَتِهِمْ لَا يَمَسُّهُمُ ٱلسُّوٓءُ وَلَا هُمْ يَحْزَنُونَ ﴿٦١﴾

62. Allah has created all things, and He is a watchful keeper over all things.

ٱللَّهُ خَـٰلِقُ كُلِّ شَىْءٍ وَهُوَ عَلَىٰ كُلِّ شَىْءٍ وَكِيلٌ ﴿٦٢﴾

63. To Him belong the keys of the heavens and the earth. Those who disbelieve in the aayaat (i.e., signs and verses) of Allah are themselves the losers.

لَّهُۥ مَقَالِيدُ ٱلسَّمَـٰوَٰتِ وَٱلْأَرْضِ وَٱلَّذِينَ كَفَرُوا۟ بِـَٔايَـٰتِ ٱللَّهِ أُو۟لَـٰٓئِكَ هُمُ ٱلْخَـٰسِرُونَ ﴿٦٣﴾

64. Say: 'Is it other than Allah you order me to worship, O ignorant ones?'

65. He did indeed reveal to you and to all those before you, that if you were to commit polytheism, your deeds would certainly become null and void, and you would indeed be among the losers.

66. Instead, just worship Allah [alone], and be among the grateful.

67. They did not form a proper estimate of Allah, like what is due to Him. The entire earth on the Day of Resurrection shall be in His grasp, and the heavens shall be rolled up in His right Hand. Exalted is He and lofty, above the partners they ascribe to Him.

68. That is when the horn shall be blown, and everyone in the heavens and everyone on earth collapses, save those whom Allah wills. Then, it shall be blown again, and all stand suddenly, looking around.

69. And the earth will then brighten by the light of its Lord. The Book will be set in place, and the prophets and witnesses are brought forth. They are judged by the truth, and they shall not be oppressed.

70. Each soul will be recompensed for what it did, as He knows best about what they had done.

71. And those who disbelieved will be driven towards Jahannam in groups. Then, when they arrive at it, its gates are opened, and its caretakers say to them: 'Did not messengers from among you come to you, reciting to you the verses of your Lord and warning you of the meeting on this day of yours?' They say: 'Of course,

but the verdict of punishment is now justly applied to the disbelievers.'

بَلَىٰ وَلَٰكِنْ حَقَّتْ كَلِمَةُ ٱلْعَذَابِ عَلَى ٱلْكَٰفِرِينَ ﴿٧١﴾

72. It is said: 'Enter through the gates of Jahannam, abiding therein forever; what a terrible abode that is for the arrogant!'

قِيلَ ٱدْخُلُوٓا۟ أَبْوَٰبَ جَهَنَّمَ خَٰلِدِينَ فِيهَا ۖ فَبِئْسَ مَثْوَى ٱلْمُتَكَبِّرِينَ ﴿٧٢﴾

73. And those who were pious unto their Lord are led towards Paradise in groups. Then, when they arrive there, its gates are [soon] opened, and its caretakers say: 'Peace be upon you! You had been good, so come inside to abide forever!'

وَسِيقَ ٱلَّذِينَ ٱتَّقَوْا۟ رَبَّهُمْ إِلَى ٱلْجَنَّةِ زُمَرًا ۖ حَتَّىٰٓ إِذَا جَآءُوهَا وَفُتِحَتْ أَبْوَٰبُهَا وَقَالَ لَهُمْ خَزَنَتُهَا سَلَٰمٌ عَلَيْكُمْ طِبْتُمْ فَٱدْخُلُوهَا خَٰلِدِينَ ﴿٧٣﴾

74. They say: 'All praise is due to Allah, the One who kept his promise and made us to inherit this place, to dwell in Paradise wherever we want! How great is the reward of those who had worked [for it]!'

وَقَالُوا۟ ٱلْحَمْدُ لِلَّهِ ٱلَّذِى صَدَقَنَا وَعْدَهُۥ وَأَوْرَثَنَا ٱلْأَرْضَ نَتَبَوَّأُ مِنَ ٱلْجَنَّةِ حَيْثُ نَشَآءُ ۖ فَنِعْمَ أَجْرُ ٱلْعَٰمِلِينَ ﴿٧٤﴾

75. And you shall see the angels encircling the throne, exalting their Lord with praise. Judgments are made between them by the truth, and it is said: 'All praise is due to Allah, the Lord of all things.'

وَتَرَى ٱلْمَلَٰٓئِكَةَ حَآفِّينَ مِنْ حَوْلِ ٱلْعَرْشِ يُسَبِّحُونَ بِحَمْدِ رَبِّهِمْ ۖ وَقُضِىَ بَيْنَهُم بِٱلْحَقِّ وَقِيلَ ٱلْحَمْدُ لِلَّهِ رَبِّ ٱلْعَٰلَمِينَ ﴿٧٥﴾

SPECIAL OPPORTUNITY!

Join in with the efforts of your brothers and sisters in South Philadelphia, as we cooperate to complete a much-needed expansion to **Masjid Ibn Baaz**. Follow the progress on X/Twitter: @mbbsouthphilly

PayPal: MasjidBinBaazPhl@gmail.com

ANSWER KEY TO THE MULTIPLE CHOICE QUIZZES & FINAL EXAM

QUIZ 1	QUIZ 2	QUIZ 3	QUIZ 4	QUIZ 5		
1. B	1. B	1. C	1. A	1. C	11. D	21. D
2. A	2. A	2. A	2. D	2. A	12. A	22. D
3. C	3. A	3. C	3. A	3. B	13. D	23. A
4. A	4. D	4. C	4. D	4. C	14. A	24. D
5. A	5. B	5. B	5. A	5. D	15. C	25. A
6. B	6. D	6. D	6. C	6. B	16. D	
7. C	7. D	7. B	7. B	7. B	17. D	
8. D	8. A	8. A	8. B	8. A	18. A	
9. D	9. A	9. C	9. C	9. D	19. A	
10. B	10. D	10. A	10. B	10. B	20. D	

وَتَرَى ٱلْمَلَٰٓئِكَةَ حَآفِّينَ مِنْ حَوْلِ ٱلْعَرْشِ يُسَبِّحُونَ بِحَمْدِ رَبِّهِمْ وَقُضِىَ بَيْنَهُم بِٱلْحَقِّ وَقِيلَ ٱلْحَمْدُ لِلَّهِ رَبِّ ٱلْعَٰلَمِينَ ۝

سُورَةُ غَافِرٍ

بِسْمِ ٱللَّهِ ٱلرَّحْمَٰنِ ٱلرَّحِيمِ

حمٓ ۝ تَنزِيلُ ٱلْكِتَٰبِ مِنَ ٱللَّهِ ٱلْعَزِيزِ ٱلْعَلِيمِ ۝ غَافِرِ ٱلذَّنۢبِ وَقَابِلِ ٱلتَّوْبِ شَدِيدِ ٱلْعِقَابِ ذِى ٱلطَّوْلِ لَآ إِلَٰهَ إِلَّا هُوَ إِلَيْهِ ٱلْمَصِيرُ ۝ مَا يُجَٰدِلُ فِىٓ ءَايَٰتِ ٱللَّهِ إِلَّا ٱلَّذِينَ كَفَرُوا۟ فَلَا يَغْرُرْكَ تَقَلُّبُهُمْ فِى ٱلْبِلَٰدِ ۝ كَذَّبَتْ قَبْلَهُمْ قَوْمُ نُوحٍ وَٱلْأَحْزَابُ مِنۢ بَعْدِهِمْ وَهَمَّتْ كُلُّ أُمَّةٍۭ بِرَسُولِهِمْ لِيَأْخُذُوهُ وَجَٰدَلُوا۟ بِٱلْبَٰطِلِ لِيُدْحِضُوا۟ بِهِ ٱلْحَقَّ فَأَخَذْتُهُمْ فَكَيْفَ كَانَ عِقَابِ ۝ وَكَذَٰلِكَ حَقَّتْ كَلِمَتُ رَبِّكَ عَلَى ٱلَّذِينَ كَفَرُوٓا۟ أَنَّهُمْ أَصْحَٰبُ ٱلنَّارِ ۝ ٱلَّذِينَ يَحْمِلُونَ ٱلْعَرْشَ وَمَنْ حَوْلَهُۥ يُسَبِّحُونَ بِحَمْدِ رَبِّهِمْ وَيُؤْمِنُونَ بِهِۦ وَيَسْتَغْفِرُونَ لِلَّذِينَ ءَامَنُوا۟ رَبَّنَا وَسِعْتَ كُلَّ شَىْءٍ رَّحْمَةً وَعِلْمًا فَٱغْفِرْ لِلَّذِينَ تَابُوا۟ وَٱتَّبَعُوا۟ سَبِيلَكَ وَقِهِمْ عَذَابَ ٱلْجَحِيمِ ۝

وَنُفِخَ فِى ٱلصُّورِ فَصَعِقَ مَن فِى ٱلسَّمَوَٰتِ وَمَن فِى ٱلْأَرْضِ إِلَّا مَن شَاءَ ٱللَّهُ ۖ ثُمَّ نُفِخَ فِيهِ أُخْرَىٰ فَإِذَا هُمْ قِيَامٌ يَنظُرُونَ ۝٦٨ وَأَشْرَقَتِ ٱلْأَرْضُ بِنُورِ رَبِّهَا وَوُضِعَ ٱلْكِتَٰبُ وَجِاْىٓءَ بِٱلنَّبِيِّـۧنَ وَٱلشُّهَدَاءِ وَقُضِىَ بَيْنَهُم بِٱلْحَقِّ وَهُمْ لَا يُظْلَمُونَ ۝٦٩ وَوُفِّيَتْ كُلُّ نَفْسٍ مَّا عَمِلَتْ وَهُوَ أَعْلَمُ بِمَا يَفْعَلُونَ ۝٧٠ وَسِيقَ ٱلَّذِينَ كَفَرُوٓا۟ إِلَىٰ جَهَنَّمَ زُمَرًا ۖ حَتَّىٰٓ إِذَا جَاءُوهَا فُتِحَتْ أَبْوَٰبُهَا وَقَالَ لَهُمْ خَزَنَتُهَآ أَلَمْ يَأْتِكُمْ رُسُلٌ مِّنكُمْ يَتْلُونَ عَلَيْكُمْ ءَايَٰتِ رَبِّكُمْ وَيُنذِرُونَكُمْ لِقَاءَ يَوْمِكُمْ هَٰذَا ۚ قَالُوا۟ بَلَىٰ وَلَٰكِنْ حَقَّتْ كَلِمَةُ ٱلْعَذَابِ عَلَى ٱلْكَٰفِرِينَ ۝٧١ قِيلَ ٱدْخُلُوٓا۟ أَبْوَٰبَ جَهَنَّمَ خَٰلِدِينَ فِيهَا ۖ فَبِئْسَ مَثْوَى ٱلْمُتَكَبِّرِينَ ۝٧٢ وَسِيقَ ٱلَّذِينَ ٱتَّقَوْا۟ رَبَّهُمْ إِلَى ٱلْجَنَّةِ زُمَرًا ۖ حَتَّىٰٓ إِذَا جَاءُوهَا وَفُتِحَتْ أَبْوَٰبُهَا وَقَالَ لَهُمْ خَزَنَتُهَا سَلَٰمٌ عَلَيْكُمْ طِبْتُمْ فَٱدْخُلُوهَا خَٰلِدِينَ ۝٧٣ وَقَالُوا۟ ٱلْحَمْدُ لِلَّهِ ٱلَّذِى صَدَقَنَا وَعْدَهُۥ وَأَوْرَثَنَا ٱلْأَرْضَ نَتَبَوَّأُ مِنَ ٱلْجَنَّةِ حَيْثُ نَشَاءُ ۖ فَنِعْمَ أَجْرُ ٱلْعَٰمِلِينَ ۝٧٤

أَوْ تَقُولَ لَوْ أَنَّ ٱللَّهَ هَدَىٰنِي لَكُنتُ مِنَ ٱلْمُتَّقِينَ ۝ أَوْ تَقُولَ حِينَ تَرَى ٱلْعَذَابَ لَوْ أَنَّ لِي كَرَّةً فَأَكُونَ مِنَ ٱلْمُحْسِنِينَ ۝ بَلَىٰ قَدْ جَآءَتْكَ ءَايَٰتِي فَكَذَّبْتَ بِهَا وَٱسْتَكْبَرْتَ وَكُنتَ مِنَ ٱلْكَٰفِرِينَ ۝ وَيَوْمَ ٱلْقِيَٰمَةِ تَرَى ٱلَّذِينَ كَذَبُوا۟ عَلَى ٱللَّهِ وُجُوهُهُم مُّسْوَدَّةٌ ۚ أَلَيْسَ فِي جَهَنَّمَ مَثْوًى لِّلْمُتَكَبِّرِينَ ۝ وَيُنَجِّي ٱللَّهُ ٱلَّذِينَ ٱتَّقَوْا۟ بِمَفَازَتِهِمْ لَا يَمَسُّهُمُ ٱلسُّوٓءُ وَلَا هُمْ يَحْزَنُونَ ۝ ٱللَّهُ خَٰلِقُ كُلِّ شَىْءٍ ۖ وَهُوَ عَلَىٰ كُلِّ شَىْءٍ وَكِيلٌ ۝ لَّهُۥ مَقَالِيدُ ٱلسَّمَٰوَٰتِ وَٱلْأَرْضِ ۗ وَٱلَّذِينَ كَفَرُوا۟ بِـَٔايَٰتِ ٱللَّهِ أُو۟لَٰٓئِكَ هُمُ ٱلْخَٰسِرُونَ ۝ قُلْ أَفَغَيْرَ ٱللَّهِ تَأْمُرُوٓنِّىٓ أَعْبُدُ أَيُّهَا ٱلْجَٰهِلُونَ ۝ وَلَقَدْ أُوحِىَ إِلَيْكَ وَإِلَى ٱلَّذِينَ مِن قَبْلِكَ لَئِنْ أَشْرَكْتَ لَيَحْبَطَنَّ عَمَلُكَ وَلَتَكُونَنَّ مِنَ ٱلْخَٰسِرِينَ ۝ بَلِ ٱللَّهَ فَٱعْبُدْ وَكُن مِّنَ ٱلشَّٰكِرِينَ ۝ وَمَا قَدَرُوا۟ ٱللَّهَ حَقَّ قَدْرِهِۦ وَٱلْأَرْضُ جَمِيعًا قَبْضَتُهُۥ يَوْمَ ٱلْقِيَٰمَةِ وَٱلسَّمَٰوَٰتُ مَطْوِيَّٰتٌۢ بِيَمِينِهِۦ ۚ سُبْحَٰنَهُۥ وَتَعَٰلَىٰ عَمَّا يُشْرِكُونَ ۝

وَبَدَا لَهُمْ سَيِّئَاتُ مَا كَسَبُوا۟ وَحَاقَ بِهِم مَّا كَانُوا۟ بِهِۦ يَسْتَهْزِءُونَ ۝ فَإِذَا مَسَّ ٱلْإِنسَٰنَ ضُرٌّ دَعَانَا ثُمَّ إِذَا خَوَّلْنَٰهُ نِعْمَةً مِّنَّا قَالَ إِنَّمَآ أُوتِيتُهُۥ عَلَىٰ عِلْمٍ ۚ بَلْ هِىَ فِتْنَةٌ وَلَٰكِنَّ أَكْثَرَهُمْ لَا يَعْلَمُونَ ۝ قَدْ قَالَهَا ٱلَّذِينَ مِن قَبْلِهِمْ فَمَآ أَغْنَىٰ عَنْهُم مَّا كَانُوا۟ يَكْسِبُونَ ۝ فَأَصَابَهُمْ سَيِّئَاتُ مَا كَسَبُوا۟ ۚ وَٱلَّذِينَ ظَلَمُوا۟ مِنْ هَٰٓؤُلَآءِ سَيُصِيبُهُمْ سَيِّئَاتُ مَا كَسَبُوا۟ وَمَا هُم بِمُعْجِزِينَ ۝ أَوَلَمْ يَعْلَمُوٓا۟ أَنَّ ٱللَّهَ يَبْسُطُ ٱلرِّزْقَ لِمَن يَشَآءُ وَيَقْدِرُ ۚ إِنَّ فِى ذَٰلِكَ لَءَايَٰتٍ لِّقَوْمٍ يُؤْمِنُونَ ۝ ۞ قُلْ يَٰعِبَادِىَ ٱلَّذِينَ أَسْرَفُوا۟ عَلَىٰٓ أَنفُسِهِمْ لَا تَقْنَطُوا۟ مِن رَّحْمَةِ ٱللَّهِ ۚ إِنَّ ٱللَّهَ يَغْفِرُ ٱلذُّنُوبَ جَمِيعًا ۚ إِنَّهُۥ هُوَ ٱلْغَفُورُ ٱلرَّحِيمُ ۝ وَأَنِيبُوٓا۟ إِلَىٰ رَبِّكُمْ وَأَسْلِمُوا۟ لَهُۥ مِن قَبْلِ أَن يَأْتِيَكُمُ ٱلْعَذَابُ ثُمَّ لَا تُنصَرُونَ ۝ وَٱتَّبِعُوٓا۟ أَحْسَنَ مَآ أُنزِلَ إِلَيْكُم مِّن رَّبِّكُم مِّن قَبْلِ أَن يَأْتِيَكُمُ ٱلْعَذَابُ بَغْتَةً وَأَنتُمْ لَا تَشْعُرُونَ ۝ أَن تَقُولَ نَفْسٌ يَٰحَسْرَتَىٰ عَلَىٰ مَا فَرَّطتُ فِى جَنۢبِ ٱللَّهِ وَإِن كُنتُ لَمِنَ ٱلسَّٰخِرِينَ ۝

إِنَّا أَنزَلْنَا عَلَيْكَ ٱلْكِتَٰبَ لِلنَّاسِ بِٱلْحَقِّ ۖ فَمَنِ ٱهْتَدَىٰ فَلِنَفْسِهِۦ ۖ وَمَن ضَلَّ فَإِنَّمَا يَضِلُّ عَلَيْهَا ۖ وَمَآ أَنتَ عَلَيْهِم بِوَكِيلٍ ۝ ٱللَّهُ يَتَوَفَّى ٱلْأَنفُسَ حِينَ مَوْتِهَا وَٱلَّتِى لَمْ تَمُتْ فِى مَنَامِهَا ۖ فَيُمْسِكُ ٱلَّتِى قَضَىٰ عَلَيْهَا ٱلْمَوْتَ وَيُرْسِلُ ٱلْأُخْرَىٰٓ إِلَىٰٓ أَجَلٍ مُّسَمًّى ۚ إِنَّ فِى ذَٰلِكَ لَءَايَٰتٍ لِّقَوْمٍ يَتَفَكَّرُونَ ۝ أَمِ ٱتَّخَذُوا۟ مِن دُونِ ٱللَّهِ شُفَعَآءَ ۚ قُلْ أَوَلَوْ كَانُوا۟ لَا يَمْلِكُونَ شَيْـًٔا وَلَا يَعْقِلُونَ ۝ قُل لِّلَّهِ ٱلشَّفَٰعَةُ جَمِيعًا ۖ لَّهُۥ مُلْكُ ٱلسَّمَٰوَٰتِ وَٱلْأَرْضِ ۖ ثُمَّ إِلَيْهِ تُرْجَعُونَ ۝ وَإِذَا ذُكِرَ ٱللَّهُ وَحْدَهُ ٱشْمَأَزَّتْ قُلُوبُ ٱلَّذِينَ لَا يُؤْمِنُونَ بِٱلْءَاخِرَةِ ۖ وَإِذَا ذُكِرَ ٱلَّذِينَ مِن دُونِهِۦٓ إِذَا هُمْ يَسْتَبْشِرُونَ ۝ قُلِ ٱللَّهُمَّ فَاطِرَ ٱلسَّمَٰوَٰتِ وَٱلْأَرْضِ عَٰلِمَ ٱلْغَيْبِ وَٱلشَّهَٰدَةِ أَنتَ تَحْكُمُ بَيْنَ عِبَادِكَ فِى مَا كَانُوا۟ فِيهِ يَخْتَلِفُونَ ۝ وَلَوْ أَنَّ لِلَّذِينَ ظَلَمُوا۟ مَا فِى ٱلْأَرْضِ جَمِيعًا وَمِثْلَهُۥ مَعَهُۥ لَٱفْتَدَوْا۟ بِهِۦ مِن سُوٓءِ ٱلْعَذَابِ يَوْمَ ٱلْقِيَٰمَةِ ۚ وَبَدَا لَهُم مِّنَ ٱللَّهِ مَا لَمْ يَكُونُوا۟ يَحْتَسِبُونَ ۝

* فَمَنْ أَظْلَمُ مِمَّن كَذَبَ عَلَى اللَّهِ وَكَذَّبَ بِالصِّدْقِ إِذْ جَاءَهُ ۚ أَلَيْسَ فِي جَهَنَّمَ مَثْوًى لِّلْكَافِرِينَ ۝ وَالَّذِي جَاءَ بِالصِّدْقِ وَصَدَّقَ بِهِ ۙ أُوْلَٰئِكَ هُمُ الْمُتَّقُونَ ۝ لَهُم مَّا يَشَاءُونَ عِندَ رَبِّهِمْ ۚ ذَٰلِكَ جَزَاءُ الْمُحْسِنِينَ ۝ لِيُكَفِّرَ اللَّهُ عَنْهُمْ أَسْوَأَ الَّذِي عَمِلُوا وَيَجْزِيَهُمْ أَجْرَهُم بِأَحْسَنِ الَّذِي كَانُوا يَعْمَلُونَ ۝ أَلَيْسَ اللَّهُ بِكَافٍ عَبْدَهُ ۖ وَيُخَوِّفُونَكَ بِالَّذِينَ مِن دُونِهِ ۚ وَمَن يُضْلِلِ اللَّهُ فَمَا لَهُ مِنْ هَادٍ ۝ وَمَن يَهْدِ اللَّهُ فَمَا لَهُ مِن مُّضِلٍّ ۗ أَلَيْسَ اللَّهُ بِعَزِيزٍ ذِي انتِقَامٍ ۝ وَلَئِن سَأَلْتَهُم مَّنْ خَلَقَ السَّمَاوَاتِ وَالْأَرْضَ لَيَقُولُنَّ اللَّهُ ۚ قُلْ أَفَرَأَيْتُم مَّا تَدْعُونَ مِن دُونِ اللَّهِ إِنْ أَرَادَنِيَ اللَّهُ بِضُرٍّ هَلْ هُنَّ كَاشِفَاتُ ضُرِّهِ أَوْ أَرَادَنِي بِرَحْمَةٍ هَلْ هُنَّ مُمْسِكَاتُ رَحْمَتِهِ ۚ قُلْ حَسْبِيَ اللَّهُ ۖ عَلَيْهِ يَتَوَكَّلُ الْمُتَوَكِّلُونَ ۝ قُلْ يَا قَوْمِ اعْمَلُوا عَلَىٰ مَكَانَتِكُمْ إِنِّي عَامِلٌ ۖ فَسَوْفَ تَعْلَمُونَ ۝ مَن يَأْتِيهِ عَذَابٌ يُخْزِيهِ وَيَحِلُّ عَلَيْهِ عَذَابٌ مُّقِيمٌ ۝

أَفَمَن شَرَحَ ٱللَّهُ صَدْرَهُۥ لِلْإِسْلَٰمِ فَهُوَ عَلَىٰ نُورٍ مِّن رَّبِّهِۦ ۚ فَوَيْلٌ لِّلْقَٰسِيَةِ قُلُوبُهُم مِّن ذِكْرِ ٱللَّهِ ۚ أُو۟لَٰٓئِكَ فِى ضَلَٰلٍ مُّبِينٍ ۝

ٱللَّهُ نَزَّلَ أَحْسَنَ ٱلْحَدِيثِ كِتَٰبًا مُّتَشَٰبِهًا مَّثَانِىَ تَقْشَعِرُّ مِنْهُ جُلُودُ ٱلَّذِينَ يَخْشَوْنَ رَبَّهُمْ ثُمَّ تَلِينُ جُلُودُهُمْ وَقُلُوبُهُمْ إِلَىٰ ذِكْرِ ٱللَّهِ ۚ ذَٰلِكَ هُدَى ٱللَّهِ يَهْدِى بِهِۦ مَن يَشَآءُ ۚ وَمَن يُضْلِلِ ٱللَّهُ فَمَا لَهُۥ مِنْ هَادٍ ۝

أَفَمَن يَتَّقِى بِوَجْهِهِۦ سُوٓءَ ٱلْعَذَابِ يَوْمَ ٱلْقِيَٰمَةِ ۚ وَقِيلَ لِلظَّٰلِمِينَ ذُوقُوا۟ مَا كُنتُمْ تَكْسِبُونَ ۝

كَذَّبَ ٱلَّذِينَ مِن قَبْلِهِمْ فَأَتَىٰهُمُ ٱلْعَذَابُ مِنْ حَيْثُ لَا يَشْعُرُونَ ۝

فَأَذَاقَهُمُ ٱللَّهُ ٱلْخِزْىَ فِى ٱلْحَيَوٰةِ ٱلدُّنْيَا ۖ وَلَعَذَابُ ٱلْءَاخِرَةِ أَكْبَرُ ۚ لَوْ كَانُوا۟ يَعْلَمُونَ ۝

وَلَقَدْ ضَرَبْنَا لِلنَّاسِ فِى هَٰذَا ٱلْقُرْءَانِ مِن كُلِّ مَثَلٍ لَّعَلَّهُمْ يَتَذَكَّرُونَ ۝

قُرْءَانًا عَرَبِيًّا غَيْرَ ذِى عِوَجٍ لَّعَلَّهُمْ يَتَّقُونَ ۝

ضَرَبَ ٱللَّهُ مَثَلًا رَّجُلًا فِيهِ شُرَكَآءُ مُتَشَٰكِسُونَ وَرَجُلًا سَلَمًا لِّرَجُلٍ هَلْ يَسْتَوِيَانِ مَثَلًا ۚ ٱلْحَمْدُ لِلَّهِ ۚ بَلْ أَكْثَرُهُمْ لَا يَعْلَمُونَ ۝

إِنَّكَ مَيِّتٌ وَإِنَّهُم مَّيِّتُونَ ۝

ثُمَّ إِنَّكُمْ يَوْمَ ٱلْقِيَٰمَةِ عِندَ رَبِّكُمْ تَخْتَصِمُونَ ۝

٤٦١

قُلْ إِنِّي أُمِرْتُ أَنْ أَعْبُدَ اللَّهَ مُخْلِصًا لَّهُ الدِّينَ ۝ وَأُمِرْتُ لِأَنْ أَكُونَ أَوَّلَ الْمُسْلِمِينَ ۝ قُلْ إِنِّي أَخَافُ إِنْ عَصَيْتُ رَبِّي عَذَابَ يَوْمٍ عَظِيمٍ ۝ قُلِ اللَّهَ أَعْبُدُ مُخْلِصًا لَّهُ دِينِي ۝ فَاعْبُدُوا مَا شِئْتُم مِّن دُونِهِ ۗ قُلْ إِنَّ الْخَاسِرِينَ الَّذِينَ خَسِرُوا أَنفُسَهُمْ وَأَهْلِيهِمْ يَوْمَ الْقِيَامَةِ ۗ أَلَا ذَٰلِكَ هُوَ الْخُسْرَانُ الْمُبِينُ ۝ لَهُم مِّن فَوْقِهِمْ ظُلَلٌ مِّنَ النَّارِ وَمِن تَحْتِهِمْ ظُلَلٌ ۚ ذَٰلِكَ يُخَوِّفُ اللَّهُ بِهِ عِبَادَهُ ۚ يَا عِبَادِ فَاتَّقُونِ ۝ وَالَّذِينَ اجْتَنَبُوا الطَّاغُوتَ أَن يَعْبُدُوهَا وَأَنَابُوا إِلَى اللَّهِ لَهُمُ الْبُشْرَىٰ ۚ فَبَشِّرْ عِبَادِ ۝ الَّذِينَ يَسْتَمِعُونَ الْقَوْلَ فَيَتَّبِعُونَ أَحْسَنَهُ ۚ أُولَٰئِكَ الَّذِينَ هَدَاهُمُ اللَّهُ ۖ وَأُولَٰئِكَ هُمْ أُولُو الْأَلْبَابِ ۝ أَفَمَنْ حَقَّ عَلَيْهِ كَلِمَةُ الْعَذَابِ أَفَأَنتَ تُنقِذُ مَن فِي النَّارِ ۝ لَٰكِنِ الَّذِينَ اتَّقَوْا رَبَّهُمْ لَهُمْ غُرَفٌ مِّن فَوْقِهَا غُرَفٌ مَّبْنِيَّةٌ تَجْرِي مِن تَحْتِهَا الْأَنْهَارُ ۖ وَعْدَ اللَّهِ ۖ لَا يُخْلِفُ اللَّهُ الْمِيعَادَ ۝ أَلَمْ تَرَ أَنَّ اللَّهَ أَنزَلَ مِنَ السَّمَاءِ مَاءً فَسَلَكَهُ يَنَابِيعَ فِي الْأَرْضِ ثُمَّ يُخْرِجُ بِهِ زَرْعًا مُّخْتَلِفًا أَلْوَانُهُ ثُمَّ يَهِيجُ فَتَرَاهُ مُصْفَرًّا ثُمَّ يَجْعَلُهُ حُطَامًا ۚ إِنَّ فِي ذَٰلِكَ لَذِكْرَىٰ لِأُولِي الْأَلْبَابِ ۝

خَلَقَكُم مِّن نَّفْسٍ وَاحِدَةٍ ثُمَّ جَعَلَ مِنْهَا زَوْجَهَا وَأَنزَلَ لَكُم مِّنَ الْأَنْعَامِ ثَمَانِيَةَ أَزْوَاجٍ ۚ يَخْلُقُكُمْ فِي بُطُونِ أُمَّهَاتِكُمْ خَلْقًا مِّن بَعْدِ خَلْقٍ فِي ظُلُمَاتٍ ثَلَاثٍ ۚ ذَٰلِكُمُ اللَّهُ رَبُّكُمْ لَهُ الْمُلْكُ ۖ لَا إِلَٰهَ إِلَّا هُوَ ۖ فَأَنَّىٰ تُصْرَفُونَ ۝٦ إِن تَكْفُرُوا فَإِنَّ اللَّهَ غَنِيٌّ عَنكُمْ ۖ وَلَا يَرْضَىٰ لِعِبَادِهِ الْكُفْرَ ۖ وَإِن تَشْكُرُوا يَرْضَهُ لَكُمْ ۗ وَلَا تَزِرُ وَازِرَةٌ وِزْرَ أُخْرَىٰ ۗ ثُمَّ إِلَىٰ رَبِّكُم مَّرْجِعُكُمْ فَيُنَبِّئُكُم بِمَا كُنتُمْ تَعْمَلُونَ ۚ إِنَّهُ عَلِيمٌ بِذَاتِ الصُّدُورِ ۝٧ ۞ وَإِذَا مَسَّ الْإِنسَانَ ضُرٌّ دَعَا رَبَّهُ مُنِيبًا إِلَيْهِ ثُمَّ إِذَا خَوَّلَهُ نِعْمَةً مِّنْهُ نَسِيَ مَا كَانَ يَدْعُو إِلَيْهِ مِن قَبْلُ وَجَعَلَ لِلَّهِ أَندَادًا لِّيُضِلَّ عَن سَبِيلِهِ ۚ قُلْ تَمَتَّعْ بِكُفْرِكَ قَلِيلًا ۖ إِنَّكَ مِنْ أَصْحَابِ النَّارِ ۝٨ أَمَّنْ هُوَ قَانِتٌ آنَاءَ اللَّيْلِ سَاجِدًا وَقَائِمًا يَحْذَرُ الْآخِرَةَ وَيَرْجُو رَحْمَةَ رَبِّهِ ۗ قُلْ هَلْ يَسْتَوِي الَّذِينَ يَعْلَمُونَ وَالَّذِينَ لَا يَعْلَمُونَ ۗ إِنَّمَا يَتَذَكَّرُ أُولُو الْأَلْبَابِ ۝٩ قُلْ يَا عِبَادِ الَّذِينَ آمَنُوا اتَّقُوا رَبَّكُمْ ۚ لِلَّذِينَ أَحْسَنُوا فِي هَٰذِهِ الدُّنْيَا حَسَنَةٌ ۗ وَأَرْضُ اللَّهِ وَاسِعَةٌ ۗ إِنَّمَا يُوَفَّى الصَّابِرُونَ أَجْرَهُم بِغَيْرِ حِسَابٍ ۝١٠

قَالَ فَالْحَقُّ وَالْحَقَّ أَقُولُ ۝ لَأَمْلَأَنَّ جَهَنَّمَ مِنكَ وَمِمَّن تَبِعَكَ مِنْهُمْ أَجْمَعِينَ ۝ قُلْ مَا أَسْأَلُكُمْ عَلَيْهِ مِنْ أَجْرٍ وَمَا أَنَا مِنَ ٱلْمُتَكَلِّفِينَ ۝ إِنْ هُوَ إِلَّا ذِكْرٌ لِّلْعَٰلَمِينَ ۝ وَلَتَعْلَمُنَّ نَبَأَهُۥ بَعْدَ حِينٍ ۝

سُورَةُ الزُّمَرِ

بِسْمِ ٱللَّهِ ٱلرَّحْمَٰنِ ٱلرَّحِيمِ

تَنزِيلُ ٱلْكِتَٰبِ مِنَ ٱللَّهِ ٱلْعَزِيزِ ٱلْحَكِيمِ ۝ إِنَّا أَنزَلْنَا إِلَيْكَ ٱلْكِتَٰبَ بِٱلْحَقِّ فَٱعْبُدِ ٱللَّهَ مُخْلِصًا لَّهُ ٱلدِّينَ ۝ أَلَا لِلَّهِ ٱلدِّينُ ٱلْخَالِصُ ۚ وَٱلَّذِينَ ٱتَّخَذُوا۟ مِن دُونِهِۦٓ أَوْلِيَآءَ مَا نَعْبُدُهُمْ إِلَّا لِيُقَرِّبُونَآ إِلَى ٱللَّهِ زُلْفَىٰٓ إِنَّ ٱللَّهَ يَحْكُمُ بَيْنَهُمْ فِى مَا هُمْ فِيهِ يَخْتَلِفُونَ ۗ إِنَّ ٱللَّهَ لَا يَهْدِى مَنْ هُوَ كَٰذِبٌ كَفَّارٌ ۝ لَّوْ أَرَادَ ٱللَّهُ أَن يَتَّخِذَ وَلَدًا لَّٱصْطَفَىٰ مِمَّا يَخْلُقُ مَا يَشَآءُ ۚ سُبْحَٰنَهُۥ ۖ هُوَ ٱللَّهُ ٱلْوَٰحِدُ ٱلْقَهَّارُ ۝ خَلَقَ ٱلسَّمَٰوَٰتِ وَٱلْأَرْضَ بِٱلْحَقِّ ۖ يُكَوِّرُ ٱلَّيْلَ عَلَى ٱلنَّهَارِ وَيُكَوِّرُ ٱلنَّهَارَ عَلَى ٱلَّيْلِ ۖ وَسَخَّرَ ٱلشَّمْسَ وَٱلْقَمَرَ ۖ كُلٌّ يَجْرِى لِأَجَلٍ مُّسَمًّى ۗ أَلَا هُوَ ٱلْعَزِيزُ ٱلْغَفَّٰرُ ۝

٤٥٨

Printed in Great Britain
by Amazon